Penguin Nature Guides

Orchids
of Northern Europe

Sven Nilsson
Illustrated by Bo Mossberg

Translated from the Swedish by H. W. Lascelles
Edited and adapted by P. Francis Hunt

Penguin Books

Penguin Books Ltd, Harmondsworth,
Middlesex, England
Penguin Books, 625 Madison Avenue,
New York, New York 10022, U.S.A.
Penguin Books Australia Ltd, Ringwood,
Victoria, Australia
Penguin Books Canada Ltd, 2801 John Street,
Markham, Ontario, Canada L3R 1B4
Penguin Books (N.Z.) Ltd, 182–190 Wairau Road,
Auckland 10, New Zealand

Nordens orkidéer first published by Wahlström & Widstrand 1977
This translation published 1979

Copyright © Bo Mossberg and Sven Nilsson, 1977
Copyright © in the English edition: Penguin Books Ltd, 1979
All rights reserved

Printed in Portugal by Gris Impressores, Cacém
Filmset in Monophoto Times by
Northumberland Press Ltd, Gateshead, Tyne and Wear

Contents

Preface

We have written this book to share our experiences of the beautiful and highly-coloured world of northern European orchids. To give our readers more general information on ecology, the biology of pollination and reproduction we have sacrificed some detailed botanical and scientific descriptions. With a few exceptions, the taxonomy and nomenclature mainly follow N. Hylander's *Nordisk kärlväxtflora II*. However, anyone who is an orchid specialist will have his own ideas about the distinctions between species and their division into sub-species. All of the illustrated orchids have been painted from living plants, almost always in their natural habitat. The right-hand pages depict the complete plant in its usual surroundings, together with details of the flower, on a scale of 1:1.

The information in the book is based on our own observations and those of others, as well as on available literature. We would like to thank the following, who have contributed so much useful help and important information: Åke Lundquist, Rolf Lidberg, Professor Bengt Pettersson, Anders Nilsson and Olof Rune, among many others.

We hope that this book helps to give a glimpse of some of nature's beautiful treasures – treasures well worth protecting. Land development, draining, trampling down and uprooting result in environmental changes that lead to the decimation or destruction of a species. Take care of our orchids!

Bo Mossberg   Sven Nilsson

Introduction

To see, to receive or to give an orchid is always a special pleasure. An orchid is unique and unusual – highly specialized in its shape, colour and growth. In all the world of plants the orchid family probably has the greatest number of species, at least 20,000. This means that nearly one in every fifteen species of flowering plant is an orchid. They exist in immense variety, from exotic, brilliant, tropical plants to the more unassuming and less conspicuous temperate species. They have always been paid special attention, not only by great scientists such as Linnaeus and Darwin, but also by many other naturalists, and interest in orchids is much wider and more specialized today than ever before. New research techniques allow us to study in greater detail the pollination procedures and vital links with fungi. Also, rapid methods have been developed for the reproduction of brilliant tropical orchids, while hybridizing has produced new shapes and colours in a very wide range of cultivated varieties.

Even though there are considerable differences between species of orchids, these differences are contained within a basically uniform structure. It is primarily the adaptation to pollinating insects which causes this seemingly inexhaustible variation on the same theme.

Despite the number of species making up the family, many orchids are comparatively uncommon and it is their rarity that contributes to their popularity. Orchids often make special demands on their environment and are therefore, in many cases, very sensitive to change. Many are threatened with extinction.

The orchids found throughout the countryside of northern Europe make up a small proportion of the total number of orchids. Here, too, there is a wide difference in appearance, method of growth, pollination procedure and environmental requirements. They are an inexhaustible subject for study, and studying them where they actually grow can be hard work, but it pays rich dividends.

The orchid family *Orchidaceae* is highly specialized among the monocotyledonous plants. It must have been one of the latest additions in the evolution of the plant kingdom. The family acquired its name from the two round tubers found underground on some of the species growing in the fields. The Greek word *orchis*, in fact, means 'testicle'. The word 'orchid' indicates that it has long been associated with folklore, popular medicine, the occult and religion. The old folk-names are often more descriptive than the modern ones.

Structure of an orchid

The structure of all orchids, expressed as adaptations to their environment, is amply reflected in the appearance of the plants. Orchids are either terrestrials (ground-dwellers) or epiphytes (tree-dwellers). Many also grow on stones (and are sometimes called epiliths) covered with lichens or moss but resemble epiphytes in their mode of growth and appearance. The epiphytic orchids are confined entirely to the tropical or sub-tropical regions but include most of those grown in greenhouses throughout the world.

Orchids vary in size from minute plants only a few millimetres tall to giants reaching several metres. Some orchids form clumps weighing several hundred kilos. Epiphytes often have thick, long and unbranched aerial roots, but in some species they are much thinner and very branched. These orchids fasten themselves to their substrate by means of their roots, and it is through them that they absorb nourishment and moisture from the air. Some of the stems are inflated and are used for storing either food or water. These somewhat onion-like stems are called bulbs or, more strictly, pseudo-bulbs, a more correct name since it is the stem that is swollen. The pseudo-bulbs can suffer considerable stress and appear quite dry after a prolonged drought, but they swell again when favourable moist conditions return. Some epiphytic orchids have a stunted stem, and the leaf, which in most species is fairly robust, can be missing. The flowers often have very bizarre shapes with very long spurs and the most striking colours.

All the species found in northern Europe are terrestrials and all are very similar in structure, at least as far as the parts which are seen above ground are concerned. The flowers arise towards the top of an ordinary leafy stalk which in the case of some tropical species can be several metres high. The leaf formation consists of ordinary green leaves, small insignificant lower sheathing leaves and coloured or green bracts subtending the flowers. The individual flowers grouped along a stem or arranged as terminal clusters are generally very small compared with those of most tropical epiphytic species, although the Venezuelan *Notylia norae* has the smallest flowers in all the family – no larger than a pin head.

Most orchids are perennial – they reappear every year. The main stem of both epiphytic and terrestrial species terminates each year's growth and continues in the following year with a new shoot from a common stem. In many ground orchids the shoot develops from a horizontal root-bearing underground stem, a rhizome, which is a food reservoir and survives the winter. Some kinds, for example *Orchis* and *Dactylorhiza* species, have tubers which survive the winter and store food. In these cases there are two round or lobe-shaped, swollen tubers similar to those found on dahlias. The one from last year is often crumpled and dark in colour, while this year's is light and filled with food. With the Fen Orchid and the Single-leaved Bog Orchid, the stem is swollen immediately above or below the surface of the ground and it has, therefore, the appearance of a pseudo-bulb. Some orchids which do not have an organ for storing food

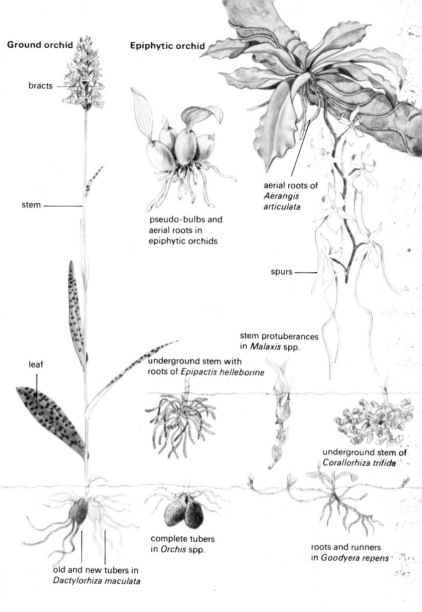

Ground orchid

bracts

stem

leaf

old and new tubers in
Dactylorhiza maculata

Epiphytic orchid

pseudo-bulbs and
aerial roots in
epiphytic orchids

aerial roots of
*Aërangis
articulata*

spurs

stem protuberances
in *Malaxis* spp.

underground stem with
roots of *Epipactis helleborine*

underground stem of
Corallorhiza trifida

complete tubers
in *Orchis* spp.

roots and runners
in *Goodyera repens*

but have a normal root system survive for long periods with the help of fungi (see p. 16). The saprophytic orchids, which live almost entirely on dead organic substances, often have a very branched root system, such as in the Coral Root and Bird's-nest Orchid.

Some orchids, for example *Goodyera repens*, form runners from the stem. These bear new shoots and the species can therefore establish itself and spread through the area without sexual reproduction.

Orchid flowers

The more simple orchid flowers bear a resemblance to lilies and certainly lilies and orchids are related to each other. Their basic structure is very similar but in lilies the perianth segments are usually identical and in orchids they are very definitely divided into an outer and an inner whorl. The orchid's outer perianth whorl comprises the three sepals, and the inner whorl the three petals, but the middle petal is always quite distinct from the other petals and from the sepals. This middle petal is called the labellum or lip. It is often produced backwards to form a nectar-containing spur which can either be insignificant or up to 30 cm long. The lip can sometimes be divided into an inner (lower) part, the hypochile, and the outer (upper) part, the epichile. During growth from the flower bud, the flower rotates through a semicircle by the twisting of the ovary or flower stalk. In this way the lip becomes directed upwards. In a number of orchids this does not happen because the bloom turns through a further half-circle.

Lilies have six stamens, the male organ of the flower, and each consists of a filament and an anther which contains the pollen. Only one stamen is found in most orchids but in certain others there are two. The stamen fuses with part of the female organs of the plant to form a combined sex organ, the column. Sometimes the sterile remains of stamens (staminodes) are found. The female organs of the flower are the pistil, which consists of the stigma (pollen acceptor) and the style, and the fruit-body which is situated at the base of the flower and attached to the stalk. In lilies there are usually three stigmas. In orchids two stigmas have merged with the stamen and the third stigma has been modified to form a special part of the column called the rostellum. This has a special function: it prevents the pollen spreading from a stamen onto the stigma of the same plant, and is of great importance in pollination (p. 14). With some exceptions, such as the Lady's Slipper, the pollen grains of orchids are collected into what is known as a pollinium. The number of pollinia varies from two to eight in every flower, depending on the species. They are usually contained in a chamber or sac in the anther of the stamen. Very often the pollinia are provided with a stem and an attached sticky disc (viscidium), which is sometimes common to two pollinia. The sticky discs can be contained in a pouch filled with liquid.

The pollen grains are very resistant to decay. Their exterior is often hard and characteristically marked. The structure of the pollen, which is easy to see in the scanning electron microscope, is of a character which can be of great importance for the systematic distinctions between and within different groups of orchids.

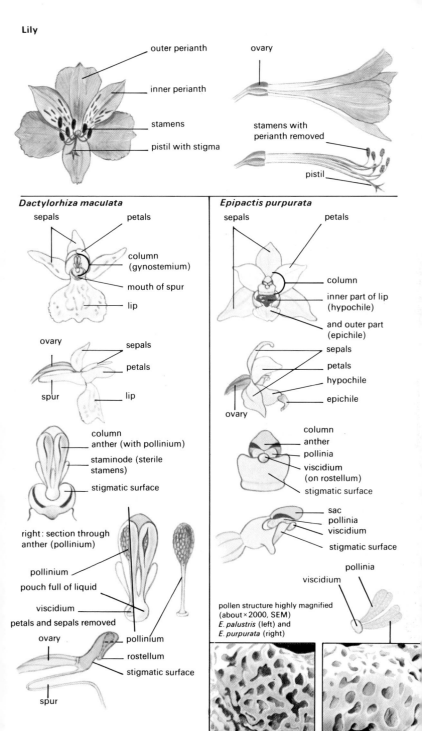

Lily

outer perianth
inner perianth
stamens
pistil with stigma

ovary
stamens with perianth removed
pistil

Dactylorhiza maculata

sepals
petals
column (gynostemium)
mouth of spur
lip

ovary
sepals
petals
spur
lip

column
anther (with pollinium)
staminode (sterile stamens)
stigmatic surface

right: section through anther (pollinium)

pollinium
pouch full of liquid
viscidium
petals and sepals removed

ovary
pollinium
rostellum
stigmatic surface
spur

Epipactis purpurata

sepals
petals
column
inner part of lip (hypochile)
and outer part (epichile)

sepals
petals
hypochile
epichile
ovary

column
anther
pollinia
viscidium (on rostellum)
stigmatic surface

sac
pollinia
viscidium
stigmatic surface

pollinia
viscidium

pollen structure highly magnified (about ×2000, SEM)
E. palustris (left) and
E. purpurata (right)

Tropical orchids

Many orchids are epiphytic and occur in tropical or sub-tropical regions. There is immense variation in their shapes, sizes, flower colours and modes of growth. The environment in which these orchids thrive is not, as is often thought, dark with stifling heat and humidity. Actually, they usually grow in tree-tops, exposed to wind, fresh air and daylight. Many of the beautiful and richly-coloured tropical species and hybrids made from them are found at the florist's and a greater number are cultivated by the amateur grower. Also, throughout the world there are many clubs and societies for orchid collectors and cultivators. However, because of their often very special propagation and growing requirements (see p. 16), many orchids can only be successfully grown and flowered in heated greenhouses. Only a very few will survive under ordinary household conditions.

A cultivated terrestrial tropical orchid was first made to flower in Europe in 1731, and in 1782 there was success with an epiphytic species. A vast number of foreign plants were brought to Europe in the late eighteenth and early nineteenth centuries. Linnaeus' pupils and other botanical explorers introduced many exotic plants, and some of these now form part of the everyday collections to be seen in botanical gardens. During the nineteenth century there was something of an orchid mania, and rare species changed hands at enormous prices. Even today some plants, especially new hybrids, are very expensive, but many are within the range of modest purses.

The epiphytic types must be cultivated indoors in Europe. Ground orchids are sometimes seen in botanical gardens, but with few exceptions they are difficult to grow, and despite their colouring are not as striking as many other hot-house plants. Those most commonly on display are the Lady's Slipper and its relatives. Ground orchids are seen to better advantage in their natural environment.

The commonest greenhouse orchids are species of Lady's Slipper, terrestrial orchids which belong to the genus *Paphiopedilum*, relatives of the European *Cypripedium calceolus*. New shapes and colours are continually bred by crossing. Species of *Cattleya* probably more than of any other genus are symbolic of orchids, or at least of the beauty of tropical orchids originating in Central and South America. By hybridizing species of *Cattleya* with those of related genera such as *Laelia*, *Schomburgkia* and *Epidendrum* a great range of flower shapes and colours have been produced. *Phalaenopsis* is another well-known genus. The white types in particular have very beautiful flowers. More recently, the genus *Dendrobium* has become popular. A common kind which we occasionally find at the florist's is the mauve *D. bigibbum* which comes from Australia. Most European countries import tropical orchids from growers in Singapore and Thailand as well as producing their own.

Dendrobium

Paphiopedilum

Phalaenopsis

Cattleya

Pollination

During the process of evolution many somewhat complicated forms of cooperation have been worked out between various forms of life. These can be seen to exist among mammals and the larger insects and in plants during the development of the mechanism of pollination. Pollination is the transfer of the male pollen to the female stigma. In self-pollination, the plant's own pollen comes in contact with the plant's own stigma, and in cross-pollination the pollen is carried from one flower to another. Cross-pollination results in cross-fruiting, the redistribution of genetic material that prevents inbreeding and degeneration. Self-pollination habitually occurs in some species but in others it only occurs as a last resort if it occurs at all.

Orchids seem to adapt their pollination processes to the carriers of their pollen – usually insects. It is even possible that co-evolution or joint evolution exists between them: the insect becomes adapted to the pollen-carrying function, while the orchid in its turn makes morphological and physiological adaptations for pollination by the insect. This complicated ecological cooperation is not easily proven, however, but we do know of some individual examples.

In many cases the flowers of an orchid are adapted to a certain group of insects or to a single type of insect. In other cases, the shape of the flower permits visits and pollination by several different types of insect. With some species a sticky mass is exploded and fastens itself to the pollinators.

Insects visit flowers for a variety of reasons: they look for food (pollen and, above all, nectar), to lay eggs, and for sexual needs. Colours, shapes and scents attract the insects. By their rotated flowers and the formation of a lip, orchids create an effective display and landing place for insects. A visit by an insect does not necessarily imply that a flower is being pollinated, however, because in many cases the pollination mechanism only operates with certain insect types. The orchids considered the most primitive have more or less loose masses of pollen held together by sticky threads, while the more advanced have the pollen aggregated into hard lumps, and the pollinia are sometimes protected by a hard waxy cover. The pollinia often have a stalk, which can be formed in different ways, which fastens onto the pollinator with the help of a sticky liquid or special sticky plates (viscidia). Even among orchids with less specialized male and female organs, there are well-adapted pollination mechanisms. For example, in the Lady's Slipper the visiting insect slips down into the large lip. Guided by the veins of the lip, it follows a series of hairs leading to the narrow exits and presses against the stamens to rub itself with pollen. When it visits another flower, the pollen comes in contact with the stigma and new pollen is transferred to the insect (see p. 24).

In older flowers which have shed their pollinia, the rostellum is bent upwards and the stigma becomes easily accessible. Similar conditions exist among the less advanced *Epipactis* species (Helleborines) whose flowers are visited and pollinated mainly by hymenopterous insects, such as bees and

Bee (*Andrena haemorrhoa*) visits *Cypripedium calceolus*

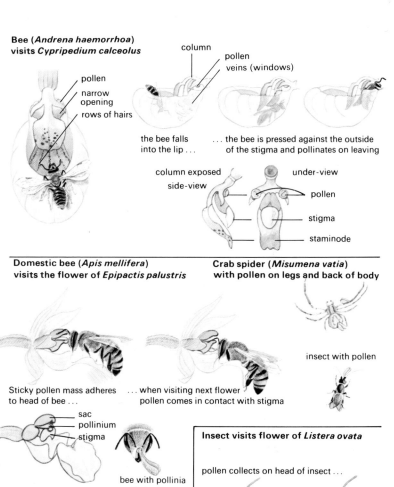

pollen
narrow opening
rows of hairs

column
pollen
veins (windows)

the bee falls into the lip . . .

. . . the bee is pressed against the outside of the stigma and pollinates on leaving

column exposed
side-view

under-view

pollen

stigma

staminode

Domestic bee (*Apis mellifera*) visits the flower of *Epipactis palustris*

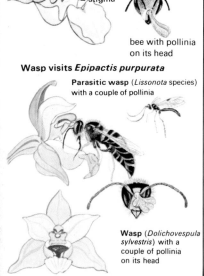

Crab spider (*Misumena vatia*) with pollen on legs and back of body

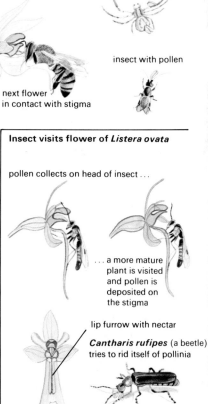

insect with pollen

Sticky pollen mass adheres to head of bee . . .

. . . when visiting next flower pollen comes in contact with stigma

sac
pollinium
stigma

bee with pollinia on its head

Wasp visits *Epipactis purpurata*

Parasitic wasp (*Lissonota* species) with a couple of pollinia

Wasp (*Dolichovespula sylvestris*) with a couple of pollinia on its head

Insect visits flower of *Listera ovata*

pollen collects on head of insect . . .

. . . a more mature plant is visited and pollen is deposited on the stigma

lip furrow with nectar

Cantharis rufipes (a beetle) tries to rid itself of pollinia

wasps. In this case the rostellum is broken and a sticky mass is set free which attaches the pollinia onto the visiting insect.

The more advanced orchids, such as *Orchis* and *Dactylorhiza* and those closely related to them, have a more specialized and highly-developed pollination mechanism. The well-developed pollinia have sticky plates, often enclosed in a pocket or pouch which is formed by the rostellum and filled with a sticky liquid. The stigma lies in a hollow beneath the stamens. The pollinators form part of the most highly-developed groups of insects with sophisticated and often very complicated behaviour patterns. The two pollinia in *Dactylorhiza* and *Orchis* species each lie in their half of the stamen. The pollen is firmly held by sticky threads combined to form a stem. The stem has an adhesive plate inside the pouch filled with liquid. An insect (bumble- or other bee), in trying to reach the spur with its sucking mouth parts, pushes up the pouch and the adhesive plates fasten themselves to the insect's head. The sticky material hardens immediately. The pollinia, which are pointed upwards, then bend forward into a position in which they can touch the stigma when the insect visits another plant. Lumps of pollen break loose from the pollinium and adhere to the stigma.

Bees and bumble-bees which are the principal pollinators seem to have suckers which accommodate to the length of the spur. Orchids with long spurs are pollinated by moths and butterflies with longer probosces. There is one kind of tropical orchid with spurs that can reach 30 cm in length, and there is one moth with an equally long proboscis. This can be regarded as an extreme case of adaptation. The Butterfly and Fragrant Orchids are examples from our native orchid flora of species pollinated by butterflies. In the Greater Butterfly Orchid, the pollinia, which are side by side, attach themselves to the insect's eyes. In the Fragrant Orchid the pollinia have a small adhesive plate which grips the sucker (see p. 80). The pollinia of the Pyramidal Orchid have a shared sticky plate which closes like a ring around the sucker of the butterfly.

In several cases specialization for pollination has gone even further. The most unusual is when the orchid flower resembles an insect and stimulates mating behaviour by shape and scent (chemically called pheromones). Such is the method used by *Ophrys*, most species of which are found in the Mediterranean region. In northern Europe we have only four species of *Ophrys* and the commonest one, the Bee Orchid (*Ophrys apifera*) is always self-pollinated. With the Fly Orchid (*Ophrys insectifera*) the male wasp (*Gorytes* species) tries to mate with the lip of the flower. The lip shape, hair formation and scent stimulate the male's mating behaviour (see p. 130). This process, called pseudocopulation, leads to the wasp removing the pollinia in its abortive attempts at mating. Groups of *Ophrys* species are restricted to the males of certain kinds or groups of wasp. In many orchids, however, there is self-pollination and therefore self-fertilization.

14–15

A moth looks for nectar in the spur of a *Platanthera chlorantha* flower

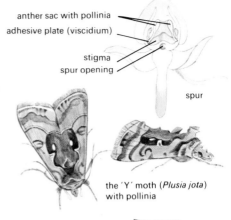

anther sac with pollinia

adhesive plate (viscidium)

stigma

spur opening

spur

when the moth puts its proboscis into the spur its head rubs against the widely-spaced pollinia

the 'Y' moth (*Plusia jota*) with pollinia

pollinia attached to the eyes of the moth

several pollinia on the Shark Moth (*Cucullia umbratica*)

Small Elephant Hawk-moth entering the flower of *Anacamptis pyramidalis*. The proboscis seeks the nectar at the base of the spur

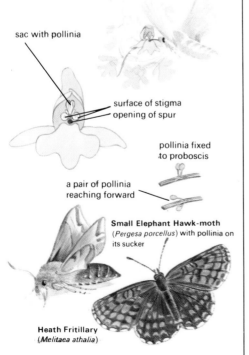

sac with pollinia

surface of stigma

opening of spur

pollinia fixed to proboscis

a pair of pollinia reaching forward

Small Elephant Hawk-moth (*Pergesa porcellus*) with pollinia on its sucker

Heath Fritillary (*Melitaea athalia*)

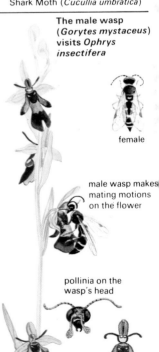

The male wasp (*Gorytes mystaceus*) visits *Ophrys insectifera*

female

male wasp makes mating motions on the flower

pollinia on the wasp's head

From seed to plant: mycorrhiza

Pollination is followed by fruiting and the formation of seeds. The pollen germinates by means of a tube which carries the male cells to the ovules in the ovary. Fruiting takes place and an embryo, the beginnings of a new plant, is soon formed. The embryo, with its protective envelope, forms the seed. Orchid seeds are very small and generally very numerous, with sometimes several millions in one fruit. The seeds lie in a capsule, a dry fruit, which, when ripe, develops long cracks and splits open. The capsules are generally attached to the plant for a long time. Sometimes the previous year's fruiting stem can be seen next to the flowers of the current year. The seeds, which are as fine as dust, usually consist of a circular central part surrounded by wing-like parts.

We have already described the complicated relationship between insects and orchids. There is also a remarkable and very close relationship between fungi and orchids. For an orchid seed to germinate under natural conditions, the presence of a fungus is necessary but even so the seeds germinate very slowly. The seeds of most plants contain some nourishment which feeds the seedling until the leaves appear and are able to produce nourishment themselves. This initial source of nourishment is not found in orchid seeds, but the germinating seed is invaded by a fungus which assists the orchid to obtain its food, and afterwards remains in the cells of the underground part of the orchid where it continues to assist in obtaining food. This type of co-existence between fungus and plant is called mycorrhiza (fungus root). The fungi are closely associated with the plant roots. In orchids, the fungus threads exist as balls in the cells of the roots or of other underground parts, the so-called endomycorrhiza (*endo*: inside). The fungus absorbs nourishment from dead organic substances in the ground. Many orchids can, for different periods of their life, grow underground with assistance from the fungus. In the case of the Burnt Orchid (*Orchis ustulata*) an underground rhizome is formed which is intertwined with the fungus threads (a mycorrhizome). It grows in segments over several years with one or more new segments appearing each year. Gradually roots appear, and a leaf-bearing plant grows. In many orchids there can be an interval of many years between the formation of the seed and the appearance of a flower. Some species depend almost entirely on a partnership with the fungus throughout their lives.

Because orchids depend on a fungus partner and their seeds are difficult to grow, cultivation and mass reproduction of the plants have been a problem. Seeds are now sown on sterilized nutrient media without the fungus partner. Recently other methods of mass propagation have been discovered: cells are excised from the plant tissue at the tips of shoots and then cultivated in a nutrient solution. An agglomeration of cells (callus) is formed and can be made to develop small embryos or sprouts (protocorms). These then develop into new plants which can be produced in very large quantities almost indefinitely.

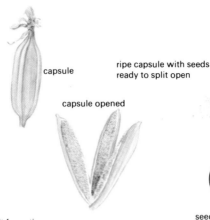

capsule

ripe capsule with seeds
ready to split open

capsule opened

seed (magnified)

ripe fruit formation
in *Dactylorhiza maculata*

root hair

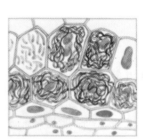

mycorrhiza in *Listera cordata* (above left)
and in *Neottia nidus-avis* (on the right);
root hairs and cells with fungal hyphae

development of rhizome in *Orchis ustulata*;
in the plant on the right, the rhizome has
been replaced by a root cluster

left: callus tissue
with protocorm
of *Paphiopedilum*

centre: bud of *Cymbidium*
for cutting out
of the growth-tissue

right: young orchid
plants in a test-tube

Ecology

Our knowledge of the ecology of native and tropical orchids is very incomplete but thanks to extensive commercial cultivation and the interest taken by amateurs in the breeding of epiphytic orchids as a hobby, most of their environmental requirements are now fairly well documented. However when it comes to the ecology of most of our own wild orchids, we know very little.

As far as their habitats are concerned, orchids often have very special requirements, and can be very sensitive to changes in the environment. On the other hand, there are certainly some species that seem to do well in the most varied environments. Terrestrial orchids seem to be the most primitive and it is likely, therefore, that the original habitat for orchids was the soil, where their association with fungi almost certainly began. The character of the soil and the presence of the fungi are the main factors in growing and propagating these orchids.

All orchids known today are associated with and dependent on fungi to a greater or lesser degree. Some fungi are specialized varieties which live only in or in association with the roots of higher plants. Others are more widely occurring, and can be parasitic. The ordinary Honey Fungus (*Armillaria mellea*) is sometimes found in partnership with orchids, a situation in which three parties are involved: the orchid depends on the fungus which in its turn is parasitic on wood.

Many of our native orchid species, like so many other orchids from the temperate and cold regions, thrive best on, or are limited to, calcareous soils. However, there are several species that thrive on acid soils and must avoid chalk, but others prefer or must have chalk. Those which occur mainly in the south seem to survive in the northern regions more easily on soil rich in chalk. Those which do not require chalk are usually more widely distributed.

A small number of terrestrial orchids seem to have become adapted to habitats disturbed by human activity. These types slowly occupy such environments, but afterwards are generally displaced by other plants. Survival can be difficult when the conditions are changed. Some types grow almost like weeds and some occur beside roads or on recently cleared ground. The Broad-leaved Helleborine which was introduced into North America spread rapidly like a weed over wide areas. Land put to different uses such as agriculture or forestry has often meant that their numbers have dwindled or they are threatened with extinction. On the other hand, others can occupy disturbed ground and flourish locally and multiply. Some tolerate considerable competition from other plants and seem to do well in close canopied shrubland or woods. As a rule, however, most orchids like a good deal of light and a regular source of moisture.

Dark pine forests support few orchids except for the Creeping Lady's Tresses, the Lesser Twayblade, Bird's-nest Orchid and Coral Root. In the more open deciduous woods are several species of *Cephalanthera* and *Epipactis*, Common Spotted Orchid, the Lady's Slipper and the Butterfly

Orchids. A few species are confined to specialized habitats such as lowland heaths, upland moors, sand dunes and limestone cliffs.

Most of our native orchids are found in open habitats: meadows, bogs, fens, marshes and downland. Hay fields and pastures that have not been too heavily grazed support plenty of orchids. Such habitats are now much less widespread, and consequently orchids are being more and more confined to spaces which man is unable to use.

There are no epiphytic species among our native orchids. Their main habitat is tropical forests where they grow on the trunks and branches of trees together with lichens, mosses and ferns. They need a suitable host plant as a place to grow, together with access to moisture and light. Water dripping from the trees, atmospheric humidity, mists and dew are absorbed by the long thick roots which also fasten the orchid to the tree. Dissolved nutrients are also absorbed from the water.

Epiphytes grow well on trees standing more or less alone on the fringes of the forests or in more open forests. Epilithic orchids, those that grow on rocks and stones, live in a similar way. The epiphytic species seem to have a greater ability to adapt than those which are confined to the ground. They often spread onto steeply sloping banks such as highway cuttings and other areas of newly-exposed soil. The seeds find it easy to grow and the young plants often come up in considerable quantities. In these places the plants normally get their water and nourishment from water oozing up to the surface and initially there is not much competition from other plants. Actually, many epiphytic orchids grow in roughly the same manner as a number of strictly ground orchids. The differences in the life pattern are therefore not very great. For instance, our native Fen Orchid (*Liparis loeselii*) and Bog Orchid (*Malaxis paludosa*) which grow among moss, are similar in appearance and growth patterns to their relatives which are found in the moss in the branches of tropical trees. The environment of the epiphytes is very much like the disturbed surroundings mentioned earlier: they have few competitors. When a tree has grown to a certain size and mosses and lichens have established themselves, the orchids follow very quickly. Cultivated trees and trees which are more exposed due to forest felling soon collect a rich epiphytic flora. Where conditions are too shady and damp, the orchids are forced out by competition from ferns and various climbers and scramblers. Where trees are exposed to strong light the conditions are very often too dry for ferns and other plants.

Orchids seem to be able to adapt very well, and can ward off pressure from man comparatively well. We still possess, here and there, very fine displays of orchids, such as in several areas in western Scotland and Ireland, where in some places there are as many orchids as the land can hold. Orchids produce great numbers of seeds and have an efficient method of distributing them, but for many tropical orchids the situation is bleak. Large areas of rain forest are being cleared and in the future many species will probably exist only in cultivation.

Over much of Europe orchids are protected by legislation from being dug up or picked, but most are being lost through the destruction or drastic alteration of suitable habitats. The setting-up of nature reserves by the government or by local groups occurs in every country, and many orchids become protected in that way. In Britain all orchids are covered by legislation from being dug up without permission of the owner of the land, and certain of the rarest species are totally protected. The latter are the Ghost Orchid, Lady's Slipper, Military Orchid, Monkey Orchid and Red Helleborine (Conservation of Wild Creatures and Wild Plants Act 1975). For a summary of the Act, see page 140.

Geographical distribution

The geographical distribution of orchids, especially tropical epiphytes, is often rather odd. A species can be widespread throughout a large area, yet be rare in some parts of it even though the climate and environmental conditions are similar. Northern orchids, too, sometimes have similar inexplicable patterns of distribution.

The distribution of a plant today depends on the climate, soil conditions and the plant's early history. Within certain species or species complexes in which stable forms have not yet become established, such as *Epipactis* and *Dactylorhiza*, new forms, varieties and species are being formed over limited areas and confuse the distribution picture. The migration history of a type as well as environmental changes within an area over a period of time contribute to the distribution pattern.

Orchids are thought to have originated during the Cretaceous period in Asia somewhere in the region of Malaya, but they are now spread throughout the world. Many of the terrestrial species are particularly widely distributed because their efficient seed dissemination, sometimes over wide areas, carries them into new regions.

Most of our native orchids are Eurasian, being widely distributed over Europe and large parts of Asia. Some of these are distinctly southern, with northern outposts here, such as the Autumn Lady's Tresses, and others are even more northerly such as Lady's Slipper and Coral Root. Some species have a purely northerly distribution range over northern Europe, Asia and America, for example the Lesser Twayblade, while some are even found in Greenland.

Some of our plants are typical of western Europe, for example the Northern Marsh Orchid (*Dactylorhiza purpurella*) with outposts in western Scandinavia. Two species, the Lapp Orchid (*Platanthera obtusata* ssp. *oligantha*) and the Arctic Orchid (*P. hyperborea*) are found high in the mountains or in the Arctic but nowhere else.

The orchids discussed in this book include those that have been found in Belgium, Channel Islands, Denmark, England, Faroes, Finland, France – northern part only, German Democratic Republic, German Federal Republic, Holland, Iceland, Ireland, Isle of Man, Luxembourg, Norway, Scotland, Sweden and Wales.

Classification of species

The *Orchidaceae* is the largest, most numerous and most highly developed of the monocotyledonous plant families. It competes with the *Compositae* (daisy family) as the largest flower family. The approximate number of species is generally put at 20,000, but figures vary between 15,000 and 30,000. This depends on the fact that many orchids have been described more than once and many others have had their names changed once or several times. Synonyms and wrong names are still used and often it is not obvious which name is the right one. The large number of cultivated varieties (cultivars) of man-made hybrids have contributed to much of the confusion in orchid names.

Orchids are often difficult plants to identify. This is partly due to their wide variation in shape and partly because they readily form hybrids with each other. It is also difficult to find an acceptable classificatory scheme for the orchid family – very many have been proposed only to be quickly neglected by most botanists. Orchids can be divided into two or three distinct families, but the most usual practice is to distinguish two or more subfamilies. The first subfamily, which is sometimes considered as a family in its own right, is considered to be more primitive than the others. In this group belong the Lady's Slipper (*Cypripedium*) and its exotic relatives of the genus *Paphiopedilum*. They have slipper-shaped lips, two fertile stamens and more or less free pollen grains. The other orchids have one fertile stamen and the pollen is agglutinated into pollinia. A summary of an orchid classification scheme is on the following page. European genera as well as some of the larger and better-known exotic ones have been included.

The orchid system

Orchidaceae		Representative genera (approximate number of species)
(*Diandrae*) with two stamens	Subfamily *Cypripedioideae* (or family *Cypripediaceae*)	*Cypripedium* (50) *Paphiopedilum* (50)
(*Monandrae*) one stamen	Subfamily *Neottioideae*	*Cephalanthera* (14) *Epipactis* (24) *Listera* (30) *Goodyera* (40) *Neottia* (9) *Spiranthes* (25)
	Subfamily *Epidendrioideae* Tribe *Epidendreae*	*Vanilla* (90) *Cattleya* (60) *Epidendrum* (400) *Malaxis* (300) *Liparis* (260) *Dendrobium* (1500) *Pleurothallis* (1000)
	Tribe *Vandeae*	*Vanda* (60) *Cymbidium* (40) *Oncidium* (350) *Calypso* (1) *Maxillaria* (300) *Odontoglossum* (200)
	Subfamily *Orchidioideae*	*Epipogium* (2) *Gymnadenia* (10) *Nigritella* (2) *Anacamptis* (1) *Coeloglossum* (2) *Platanthera* (200) *Orchis* (35) *Dactylorhiza* (30) *Habenaria* (600) *Chamorchis* (1) *Disa* (130) *Ophrys* (30) *Herminium* (30)

Cypripedium calceolus

L. (*Kypris*: Aphrodite, *pedilon*: shoe, *calceolus*: small shoe)

Lady's Slipper

Our largest and most exotic-looking orchid. Scrubby fields and copses are the natural habitat of the Lady's Slipper, but it also does well in open marshland and in woods and is found almost exclusively on calcareous soil. As a rule it grows in small groups. Flowers appear in June or July and last for about a fortnight. They grow singly or in twos and threes on the upper part of a broad-leafed stalk which starts below the ground as a runner and can reach a height of about 45 cm. The size and colour of the flowers makes them easy to see from a long distance. The inflated yellow slipper-like lip contrasts markedly with the small twisted red-brown petals. The flowers have a nice smell, but no nectar. Their strange construction seems to be an adaptation to pollination. The lip's opening has smooth indented sides, on the inside of which are rows of hairs converging at the base of the lip. Transparent folds or 'windows' are on both sides of the lip. The lip is a trap for insects, including the pollen-collecting bee of the genus *Andrena*. A visiting bee loses its foothold on the smooth side of the lip, drops in, and cannot escape. With the help of the 'window' it notices the narrow exit beneath the stamens. On the way out, the pollen it carries is deposited on the stigma and new pollen collects on the bee's back. The insect, worn out by its five- to ten-minute imprisonment, which has consumed a lot of its energy, soon drops into another flower (see p. 13).

The genus to which the Lady's Slipper belongs includes about fifty other species, spread mainly over the cool and temperate regions of the northern hemisphere. Our native Lady's Slipper is a north Eurasian species. The North American Lady's Slipper is sometimes regarded as a variety of ours, sometimes as a distinct species.

Because of its beauty and size, the Lady's Slipper has been extensively picked, which is why it has disappeared in all but one of its former locations in England. This solitary locality in Yorkshire is well protected, and during the plant's flowering season it has a day-long guard to prevent picking or digging. Attempts are being made to obtain seed from one of the two plants remaining to see if it can be propagated by the latest laboratory techniques. However, it is still quite frequently seen in gardens, but these plants have all been obtained from mainland Europe.

slipper-like lip
with column at top

Cephalanthera rubra

(L.) L. C. Rich.   (*kephale*: head, *anthera*: stamen, *rubra*: red)

Red Helleborine

Cephalanthera and *Epipactis* are closely related genera and together constitute a group of orchids whose flower structure and pollination biology seem to be very primitive. The lip consists of two parts, an upper and a lower. The spur is missing (see p. 8). The upper part of the lip of the Red Helleborine is flat; the lower part is boat-shaped, making the flower resemble a bell or tube. It stands on a thin spike on a base of green supporting leaves stemming from a some-what zig-zag-shaped stalk. This grows from a runner deep in the ground. The spear-shaped leaves are generally spaced at regular intervals along the entire stalk. The beautiful Red Helleborine with its large magenta pink or pink-violet flowers blooms in June or early July. Like others in the species it has no nectar. The single stigma is sticky, and any visiting insect, such as a bee, becomes sticky along its body. The pollen, which is directed forward and is not on a stem, can therefore be transferred to the back of the insect as it leaves the flower. Self-pollination at the bud stage has also been observed. The Red Helleborine grows in several types of woodland, prefer-ably on cleared ground, and usually on alkaline soil.

The sudden disappearance or appearance of the flower in a locality can be explained by its vigorous mycorrhizal activity (see p. 16). If the locality becomes too shaded or overgrown because of, for example, afforestation, few or no leaves are formed and the plant must depend entirely on fungi for its nourishment. Food is stored in the roots of underground shoots which form tubers from which, in due course, new plants grow. The Red Helleborine can grow for a long time without putting shoots above the ground. If the circum-stances change in its favour, for example by tree felling, new shoots can form and produce flowers.

The Red Helleborine occurs throughout Europe, ex-tending eastwards through the Middle East to Iran. In the British Isles *Cephalanthera rubra* occurs today only in the Chiltern and Cotswold Hills in England and on its sites there it is very rare. Formerly it extended into adjoining areas and was much commoner, but overpicking of the striking flowers in the past and trampling by orchid-seekers today has led to its virtual extinction.

Cephalanthera longifolia

(L.) Fritsch (*longifolia*: with long leaves)

Narrow-leaved Helleborine

This stately Narrow-leaved or Sword-leaved Helleborine, with its clear white flowers, is one of our most decorative and striking orchids. In Denmark and Norway it is known as the White Lady. Its habitat is mostly in deciduous and scrubby woodland margins, but recently it has migrated into more open country, for example, abandoned pastureland, or recultivated meadowland. It also occurs in other very different surroundings: in sand dunes, swampy ground, pastures and open pine woods. It seems to require less calcareous soil than the Red Helleborine and the White Helleborine, but it is more dependent on moisture. It differs in appearance from these in its well-arranged compact inflorescence which is rich in blooms. The supporting leaves are fairly short, and are very different from the other long and narrow leaves on the stalk which can grow to as much as 45 cm. Each inflorescence can have as many as ten or twenty blooms, sometimes more. The flowers open out more than those on the White Helleborine.

The Narrow-leaved Helleborine flowers from mid-May to the beginning of July. The honey-bee, wild bee and wasp have been observed on the flowers, and it is supposed that they are involved in pollination. The method seems to be the same as with the Red Helleborine but it is thought that there is some self-pollination as well. Seed production can therefore be poor and irregular with poor access to the pollinia. As a rule, very few seed pods are seen. The Narrow-leaved Helleborine withers and sets its seeds earlier than the other kinds, which, along with other factors, gives it a better chance of remaining in hay fields. The roots of the ground runners are of two kinds, either thickened in places and storing food without association with the fungal mycelium, or long and thin with very pronounced mycorrhizal activity. Tubers can form from the roots, but they are not as important in the propagation of the Narrow-leaved Helleborine as they are for the Red Helleborine.

The Narrow-leaved Helleborine is more widely spread than the other species of *Cephalanthera*. It extends southwards through Europe to North Africa and eastwards to the Himalayas and western China. In some parts of Europe it has spread recently because of changes in the use of the ground, and it sometimes grows together with the Red Helleborine and White Helleborine. Hybrids have been found. *Cephalanthera longifolia* is found throughout the British Isles but is nowhere common, probably because there are few suitable sites that have not been destroyed by over-cultivation or deforestation.

fruiting stem

Cephalanthera damasonium

(Mill.) Druce   (*damasonium*: plant name in Pliny, *damazo*: to allay or heal)

White Helleborine

The White Helleborine does not create such a striking impression as the regal Narrow-leaved Helleborine. This is partly because there are generally fewer flowers and they do not contrast as strongly with the foliage and their leafy bracts which partly hide the flowers. The White Helleborine can grow in drier country than the other species. In fully-developed plants the thick roots run deep into the soil from the erect ground stem. In contrast with the fine horizontal system of young plants, they almost never have a fungus partner. Recently, the White Helleborine has spread to new localities in some parts of Europe. Because it thrives in rather shaded surroundings, often on stony and mossy ground in woods and among shrubs, it is thought to favour areas where the ground has been put to a new use such as the growth of shrubs.

The inflorescence of the White Helleborine generally has few flowers, but occasionally as many as fifteen are found. The few broad, short, spear-shaped leaves change in succession into the support leaves which become smaller towards the top of the grouping. The grey-white, sometimes pure white blooms are closer together than in the Narrow-leaved Helleborine. Both types have ochre-yellow ridges on the upper part of the lip. The plant only flowers after it is about ten years old, and the flowering time is from mid-May and through June to early July. In many parts of Europe, bumble-bees and ordinary bees visit the plants, but pollination with the help of insects is thought to be rare. Instead, the White Helleborine is, as a rule, self-pollinating, and this easily happens by its own pollen falling onto the stigma.

The White Helleborine is found mostly in southern and central Europe and it has spread east to eastern Russia and south to North Africa. The most northerly outposts are the Swedish occurrences in Gotland. In the British Isles *Cephalanthera damasonium* is confined to southeast and central southern England but can occur in substantial populations in those areas, especially in chalky areas at the edge of woods or sometimes, even, under the heavy shade of beech woods.

C. rubra *C. longifolia* *C. damasonium*

Epipactis atrorubens

(Hoffm.) Schult. (*epipactis*: name for lily growth having similar leaves, *atrorubens*: dark red)

Dark-red Helleborine

Among the tall orchids are species of the Helleborine group *Epipactis*. They are easily noticed because they come into flower at the end of July or early August, somewhat later than most other orchids. Their growing habits, leaf appearance and two-part lip indicate that they are related to the *Cephalanthera* species. The flowers, which are more open, grow on an upright stem with short bracts in a compact, well-defined inflorescence. A slit divides the lip which consists of an inner (lower) cup-shaped part containing nectar, and an outer (upper) part which is curled, indented or with a protrusion. Some of the species are scented. In types pollinated by insects, the pollinia are fastened onto a special part of the rostellum (see p. 13) by means of a sticky mass.

It is difficult to distinguish between a considerable number of the twenty-five members of this genus, and many of them should be referred to a specialist for identification.

One can come across the Dark-red Helleborine with its strong wine or purple colour – or even brownish dark red – in limestone areas on exposed cliffs and screes, among ash scrub or open ground. It also grows in sparse stony or sandy scrub, on stony beaches and nearly always on dry land exposed to the sun. It does not seem to be wholly dependent on its fungus partner. The thick tall stalk, with a cluster of hairs on the upper part, rises from a short underground stem. The leaves are wide and short and, like the stalk, are often a pronounced violet. The blooms hang on one side in a long narrow inflorescence. The flowers appear at the height of the summer. Bumble-bees visit the vanilla-scented flowers. The pollinia, which fall onto a shelf above the stigma, are pulled out with the help of the sticky mass on the rostellum, and attach themselves to the insect's forehead.

E. atrorubens, which in some books is referred to as *E. atropurpurea* Raf., grows over a wide area of Europe, and eastwards to Siberia and central Asia. The Dark-red Helleborine is rare in the British Isles, being found in very small numbers in scattered localities in northern Wales, northern England, northwest Scotland and central western Ireland.

32–33

Epipactis helleborine

(L.) Crantz   (*helleborus*: a treatment for lunacy or epilepsy)

Broad-leaved Helleborine

This orchid, often camouflaged because of its green flowers, is among the taller species. Its habitat is in deciduous and evergreen woods, sometimes fairly common over wide areas, but it is unusual for more than a few plants to be found together.

The Broad-leaved Helleborine shows wide ecological variations. It can be found in many widely differing habitats, often in quite acid areas. With the aid of mycorrhiza it can grow even in very sheltered surroundings and can live for long periods beneath the ground. The appearance of the plant often varies with the habitat. In the shade, the growth is similar to the Green-flowered Helleborine – slender and pale green – while on ground exposed to the sun it is more like the Dark-red Helleborine – thicker and redder.

The rhizome is short with short nodes and rather thick roots. The stalk tends to be short with thin spread-out leaves all around it. On soft ground the plant is closely bound up with its fungus partners. The open blooms, which are directed out and down, form a long compact inflorescence with sometimes as many as a hundred blooms. The flower colours are very varied – some parts can have combinations of green, red, pink and purple. The wide upper (outer) part of the lip is often bent down and back. The plant flowers late, from the end of July to the end of August. Effective pollination is mainly by wasps, but the blooms are also visited by other insects including the bumble-bee and the ordinary bee. It is said that the nectar and the many-flowering root clusters, like some other plants, may be poisonous or have a narcotic effect (see p. 36).

Many sub-species and varieties of this species have been described, but it is not certain whether these diverging types are really genetically distinct. The Broad-leaved Helleborine is widespread throughout Europe and extends southwards to North Africa and eastwards to Siberia and the Himalayas. In Britain it is one of our commoner and more widely-spread species and is found in suitable habitats in all areas except the northeast tip of Scotland. It is unlike many of our other wild orchids in that it usually grows in large clusters.

Closely related to *Epipactis helleborine* is the very rare Dune Helleborine *E. dunensis* (T. & T. A. Steph.) Godf. a smaller and generally duller plant occurring only in dune-slacks in coastal areas of northern England and Anglesey.

fruiting stem

bud stage

Epipactis purpurata

G. E. Sm.   (*purpurata*: purple-coloured)

Violet Helleborine

The Violet Helleborine is not very widespread in Europe. It
has been reported only from England, Denmark, Switzer-
land, France, Germany, Austria and Russia, but probably
has been overlooked or confused with the Broad-leaved
Helleborine. As a rule it likes the shade, and is usually found
in beech woods on calcareous soil, as well as in clay soil in
hazel thickets and the edge of woods, although it is rare in
open ground. In the woodlands, with the leaf-covered ground
and where the light is poor, it is sometimes the only plant
to be found. Characteristic of this species is the fact that
several stems can grow from the same point on the stout
rhizome which lies unusually deep under the surface. The
stems, which can sometimes be a metre tall and comparatively stout, bear a compact inflorescence. The grey-green
leaves are rather narrow with a pronounced violet tinge.
The open flowers have pointed perianth segments which
are greenish-white with a slight reddish tinge. The inner
cup-shaped part of the lip is purple on the inside and the
outer part is white. The plant flowers very late, generally
in August, and sometimes even in September. Like the
Broad-leaved Helleborine it is pollinated mainly by wasps
and is said to have a poisonous or narcotic nectar. The
large compact inflorescences are also visited by other insects
(see p. 13). One investigator said that the attractive nectar
made the wasp 'drunk' and therefore less energetic in
scraping away the pollinia accumulated on his head. It is
possible that this effect comes from the yeast fungi found in
the nectar, which probably puts the insect completely 'under
the influence' of alcohol.

fruiting stem

Can this plant, with its narrow coloured leaves, produce
enough food in an environment where the light is poor? Some
forms are entirely red-violet and contain no chlorophyll.
One theory is that the orchid has a partly saprophytic
growth pattern and depends almost entirely on its fungus
partner. Another is that the plant has efficient deep-lying
roots, so far not associated with any fungus.

The Violet Helleborine has sometimes been regarded as a
variety or sub-species of the Broad-leaved Helleborine. However, it has also been recorded growing in sandy soil. It
extends to southern and central Europe as well as some parts
of western Siberia. In Britain *E. purpurata* has only been
reliably recorded from southeast England and the southern
Midlands.

36–37

Epipactis leptochila

Godf.   (*leptochila*: with narrow lip)

Narrow-lipped Helleborine

This orchid, which is nowhere very common, grows on calcareous soil in deciduous woods, especially in beech and oak woods, and there are also a few records of its occurrence on sand dunes. In 1921 it was described as a species in its own right, but is still considered by some naturalists as being no more than a sub-species or ecological form of the Broad-leaved Helleborine. Its flowers, however, are different and it is self-pollinating. There are no red markings and the plant looks yellow-green to olive green. The conspicuously hairy stalk carries two rows of yellow-green leaves with prominent veins. It generally grows singly from a long thick rhizome.

The slightly drooping flowers are spaced rather widely, and are comparatively large and wide open. The Latin name *leptochila* indicates that the outer part of the lip, which is indented at the base, is long and pointed and not bent as with *Epipactis helleborine*. The inner part of the lip is dark on its inner surface. The plant flowers at the end of July and in August. It is probable that, like the Green-flowered Helleborine, it is self-pollinating, but there is evidence for supposing that sometimes pollination is with the help of insects. The rostellum is smaller, and the stamen, which has a large stalk, is inclined forwards. The pollinia fall apart and easily drop onto the stigma. Seed set is usually good and the resulting fruit with its relatively large seed pods is very striking. It is not clear whether the self-pollination in this and perhaps other species is a result of a continuing atrophy of the rostellum which eventually will lose its function completely. Like several other species in the genus, *Epipactis leptochila* has certainly been overlooked, and too little is known about its occurrence even in the British Isles. However, mainly through the pioneer work of the late Dr D. P. Young, who specialized in epipactology, it has been found in several parts of Europe as far apart as Denmark and Greece. Although they have not been recorded in the British Isles there are three other species of Helleborine that recently have been reported from northern Europe, *E. confusa*, *E. microphylla* and *E. mulleri*.

Epipactis phyllanthes

G. E. Sm.   (*phyllanthes*: indicates the leaf-like perianth)

Green-flowered Helleborine

E. helleborine

This species is one of the many orchids closely related to the Broad-leaved Helleborine. In the past it was considered merely a variety of *Epipactis helleborine* but Dr D. P. Young, the English epipactologist, has clarified its taxonomic status as an amply distinct species with several well-defined local variations. These have been named as follows: var. *cambrensis* (C. Thom.) D. P. Young (south Wales, sand dunes); var. *degenera* D. P. Young (southern England, woods); var. *pendula* D. P. Young (northwest England, north Wales, woods and dunes); var. *phyllanthes* (southern England, woods) and var. *vectensis* (T. & T. A. Steph.) D. P. Young (southern England, southern Wales, woods). The differences between these varieties are concerned with small but fairly consistent floral features, but the picture is never very clear as many intermediate forms have been reported.

E. phyllanthes

E. phyllanthes is thus a very variable species and these variations are probably connected with self-pollination. This narrow, often pale green orchid, has a leafless or almost leafless stalk which grows from a short rhizome with thick roots, and bears short, delicate, oval, spear-shaped leaves. The hanging blooms vary in appearance according to the variety – in some cases they are closed and bell-like, in others they are more open. The perianth is always pale green and pointed but the lip can be quite variable. The lower part is sometimes very distinct but in some plants it is almost indistinguishable from the rest of the flower. The outer part of the lip has a white tip and reddish-white indentations at the base. The circumstances surrounding pollination have not been fully explained, but self-pollination seems to be the normal method. This sometimes occurs when the bloom is in the bud stage, and then ripe seed pods are found almost as soon as the flowers are in bloom.

left: *E. helleborine*
right: *E. phyllanthes*

The Green-flowered Helleborine grows in chalk and limestone regions in a great range of habitats: deciduous woods, pine woods, thickets and woodland margins. Sometimes it is found on very dry sandy soil, sometimes on land which can be flooded. The extent of its distribution outside the British Isles is not well known, but careful exploration in likely habitats and equally careful examination of likely specimens has led to it being recognized in Sweden and Denmark. It will no doubt be found eventually in many other places.

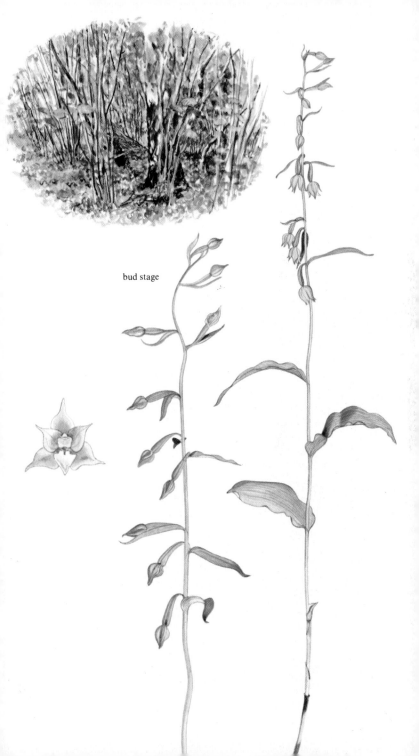

bud stage

Epipactis palustris

(L.) Crantz   (*palustris*: grows in marshes)

Marsh Helleborine

The Marsh Helleborine is probably the finest of the *Epipactis* species. Large numbers in a marsh, all in full flower, are a striking sight. As the large flowers nod gently in the wind, their contrasting colours become very obvious. In contrast with the other species, the Marsh Helleborine has a very branched underground rhizome from which develops the slightly hairy flowering stem. The flowers are arranged in loose clusters with the perianth hanging freely on the fruit-body which is bent backwards. The outer perianth is a pale brownish red and the inner one is white. The lip dominates with its broad, white, curled outer part. Its connection to the inner trough-shaped part, which has two ear-like extensions, is flexible. There is a form of the plant which lacks all red pigment: it is generally considered as a variety *ochroleuca* Barla. Flowers usually develop in July which is earlier than with most other *Epipactis* species. This orchid is visited and pollinated by many different insects; bees, flies, beetles and even ants and spiders have been seen inside the flowers. The insects, which seem to be efficient pollinators, get the pollinia fastened onto them when they withdraw from the flower, having tripped over part of the lip.

The Marsh Helleborine can spread quickly over large areas by means of its creeping underground shoots and sometimes produces several hundred flowering stems. It has fairly large seeds which readily float on water and thus the plant can spread to new localities. The plant occurs mainly in fens, marshes, damp fields, dune-slacks and other sandy ground, but it occasionally migrates into different habitats, especially newly-exposed ground such as abandoned gravel pits and earthworks.

The Marsh Helleborine is found throughout Europe and extends far into temperate Asia and North Africa. However, like so many species of the wetlands, it has disappeared from much of its range because of the ever-increasing destruction and degradation of suitable habitats by drainage and pollution. In the British Isles, although it is nowhere as common as it was even fifty years ago, it can still be found throughout England, Wales, Scotland and Ireland.

Epipogium aphyllum

G. E. Sm.   (*epi*: on, *pogon*: beard [lip], *aphyllum*: leafless)

Ghost Orchid, Spurred Coral Root

This orchid appears suddenly, only to disappear just as quickly, for many years. In the British Isles it is very rarely encountered having been found in less than a dozen localities since its first discovery in 1854. It has not been seen in its former Welsh border sites since the first decade of this century, but in the woods above Marlow along the middle reaches of the Thames river it is now recorded every year. The explanation is to be found in its saprophytic life-style and the special development of its shoots. It is devoid of chlorophyll, being entirely dependent on its fungus partner for all nourishment. The underground rhizome, which resembles coral, bears fine hairs through which the fungi can penetrate. Some of the branches of the rhizome develop into buds which in the autumn contain the makings of a flower for next year. If the following spring weather is kind, these shoots will emerge as flowers. Many observations indicate that flowering takes place after a damp and mild spring. If the spring is not kind, then the young shoots die before emerging, but the rhizome will continue to grow. On the European mainland the plant is capable of spreading over very wide areas by means of long thin runners. Tubers form on these runners, which gradually separate, and after a number of years a new plant will develop from them. After flowering, the shoot and parts of the ground stem die and it can take up to ten years before the plant flowers again, but this may be in a different place.

Flowering takes place in August. The brittle, fragile and almost transparent stalks carry filmy leaves with a pale red tinge and a few large flowers with transparent yellow-white perianths. The lip, shaped like a cloverleaf, has a whitish central lobe with red-violet markings. The thick red-white spur rests against its reverse side. The flowers have a pleasant scent. It is known that bumble-bees visit the flowers, but very little is known about the detailed processes of pollination. Seeds are rarely produced, but the species generally has recourse to its ability to propagate and spread beneath the ground.

In most of northern Europe it is found mainly in the pine forests, but in the more southern parts it is an inhabitant of beech and oak woods. It has also been encountered in birch woods in some mountainous areas. Its total distribution extends to the whole of Europe, throughout temperate Asia eastwards to Japan, the Himalayas and northern India.

Listera ovata

(L.) R. Br. (*Listera*, after the English scientist M. Lister, *ovata*: oval, indicating the leaf shape)

Twayblade

As far back as the early years of the nineteenth century many gardeners were saying that the Twayblade deserves 'a place in pleasure gardens among the trees'. This orchid is not particularly striking but the two large oval leaves and the tall stalk certainly mean that people notice it. However, the yellow-green flowers are quite inconspicuous against the fresh spring greenery of the woodland floor or the tall downland grasses. It is naturally at home in these environments, but it is not particularly fastidious about its growing areas as it can also be found in marshes and fens and on many roadside and railway verges.

The plant normally has two leaves placed opposite each other and situated below the centre of the stalk, but occasionally the leaves are not strictly opposite or there may be one or three leaves instead of two. The Twayblade has a rhizome and long roots which are in part food-retaining. The flowering stem, which can grow to about 45 cm, is sticky with glands and carries a long narrow inflorescence. The flowers have a long bilobed lip which hangs downwards and the petals and sepals form a hood-like structure so that the whole flower has a rather fanciful humanoid appearance.

Flowers appear over a long period, beginning in the spring and continuing well into July. A large variety of insects, including flies and beetles, are thought to visit the musk-scented flowers and are responsible for the pollination (see p. 13). The insect crawls up along the lip which has a nectar channel in a long shiny ridge. Gradually the insect reaches the rostellum which almost explodes a sticky liquid. The ripening pollinia are deposited on the rostellum and can easily attach themselves to the insect's head. In older flowers the rostellum is bent upwards and the stigma is exposed. In these flowers the pollinia from a visiting insect can easily attach themselves to the stigma. When the stamen in a flower yields its pollen before the stigma is ready to receive it, self-pollination is made difficult, and therefore it is the pollen from young plants which is deposited on the old ones. The Twayblade's erect seed pods open in damp weather when touched.

The Twayblade often grows in large quantities over wide areas and is easily the most common European orchid. *Listera ovata* is found everywhere in the British Isles except on the bleaker mountains and more acidic-soil heaths and moorlands and in highly industrialized and urbanized areas. Despite the effects of increasingly intensive agriculture and the ravages of flower pickers and tramplers, it is often seen at the edge of arable fields, in grazing pastures and growing thickly in public open spaces.

fruiting stem

46–47

Listera cordata

(L.) R. Br.   (*cordata*: heart-shaped)

Lesser Twayblade

Many people imagine that orchids are always striking and colourful, but this is not always the case. The slender inconspicuous Lesser Twayblade often escapes even the attentive field botanist since it grows concealed in the vegetation. As a rule it is only about 15 cm tall. The graceful stem, sometimes tinged with red, with its two small heart-shaped shining leaves, grows from a thin, creeping, short-lived rhizome. The lax inflorescence bears pale purple-green flowers. The lip is markedly bilobed at the tip with outward-bending lobes. It lacks the separate nectar channel of the ordinary Twayblade. Very little is known of its pollination biology, but small insects such as flies and small hymenoptera have been suggested as pollinators and there can also be self-pollination. Seed formation takes place quickly, and it is possible to find plants with inflorescences at the base of which there is the characteristic spherical ripe seed pod but with the apical flowers only just opened.

The Lesser Twayblade can multiply and spread efficiently with the aid of its underground stem and root system. Some roots can form tubers which develop into new plants. Since the underground stems are soft, have few roots and hardly any food store, the Lesser Twayblade is very largely dependent on its mycorrhizal partner throughout its entire life. This orchid survives well in soil which is poor in nourishment, particularly in upland pine woods. It is also found in deciduous birch woods and sometimes in small bogs where it grows alongside more typical bog plants such as sundew. Occasionally it grows on heaths and moorlands where it is completely hidden in the heather and other dwarf shrubs. In contrast to the common Twayblade, it occurs singly or in small scattered groups.

Listera cordata is circumpolar, extending throughout northern and central Europe and Asia, southern Greenland and large areas of North America. In the British Isles it has a markedly western and northern distribution and is particularly common in northwest Scotland although there are isolated records from Exmoor in Somerset and Devon. As it can be so inconspicuous it should be sought in any likely area in Scotland where it is often found right in the centre of an old heather plant.

Neottia nidus-avis

(L.) L. C. Rich.   (*neottia*: nest, *nidus-avis*: nest, indicative of the root system)

Bird's-nest Orchid

Many who see the Bird's-nest Orchid for the first time assume that it is a withered plant, a winter stem remaining from last year. But it is actually a remarkable feature of the woods – pale yellow-brown in the midst of all the green growth. Under the soil its unique root system resembles a magpie's nest with numerous thick roots growing from a short ground shoot. The sturdy stem, not unlike asparagus, grows to about 25–40 cm and bears stunted translucent brown leaves. The inflorescence is clustered at the top, but thins out at the bottom. In relation to the other parts of the flower the lip is large and has outward-hanging lobes which are most conspicuously developed in the lower flowers. At the base there is a cavity which produces a weakly honey-scented nectar which attracts a large number of insects, mostly flies. The Bird's-nest Orchid flowers from the beginning of May. Very little is known about its method of pollination, but it is thought that self-pollination is the most usual. Sometimes the flower buds develop under a cover of moss, or even completely underground. Because of the habitual self-pollination these flowers readily set seeds. Seed production is efficient as can be seen from the characteristic infructescences which often remain in place until after the flowers of the next season have appeared.

When the Bird's-nest Orchid has flowered, the underground rhizome and some of the root system generally die. Meanwhile, some of the roots form new shoots at the tip, which is how the plant can spread and is propagated underground. Investigations have shown that there is chlorophyll in the plant, but it is mainly used for food absorption with the help of the fungus partner. The fungus forms enzymes which help the roots to absorb substances from the humus. The Bird's-nest Orchid is also a saprophyte, and lives on decayed material from plants and animals. It is therefore most at home in soft earth in damp deciduous and pine forests.

Our own *Neottia nidus-avis* occurs throughout central and northern Europe and eastwards through Siberia, the Caucasus and Asia Minor. Although in many parts of its range it survives well at altitudes up to 2,000 m, in the British Isles it is decidedly a lowland species, particularly widespread in beech woods on the chalk of southern England. Nevertheless it has been recorded from almost every county.

Similar in its overall appearance but much larger and suffused violet throughout is the Violet Bird's-nest Orchid [*Limodorum abortivum* (L.) Sw.] which occurs in coniferous woods in parts of France and Germany.

fruiting stem

50–51

Goodyera repens

(L.) R. Br. (*Goodyera* after the seventeenth-century English-man John Goodyer, *repens*: creeping)

Creeping Lady's Tresses

The Creeping Lady's Tresses is an orchid of mossy wood-lands. One can suddenly discover this completely unsuspected plant when picking bilberries and whortleberries. Its long rhizome creeps in or beneath the moss covering. The dark green leaves with their network of paler nerves are probably its most outstanding characteristic. The leaves form a rosette at the base of the stalk. The more or less one-sided and spiked inflorescence is pale yellow-green with short hairs and slightly bent back at the top. The small, elegant, sweetly-scented flowers are white, and the sepals have a mass of glandular hairs. The lip has an outer pointed part resembling a tongue, and an inner part similar to a pouch or cup partitioned off from the nectar. The orange-red parts of the reproductive organ are in marked contrast to the white sepals and petals. It is thought that pollination is carried out by the bumble-bee. The flower, when newly opened, is somewhat tubular and only the pollinia can be reached by the head of a visiting insect, but later it opens up and the stigma becomes exposed and more accessible. The plant is in flower from the beginning of July until about the middle of September.

The seeds of the Creeping Lady's Tresses are very small and as fine as dust. Even if seed formation does not occur, the plant can spread and propagate with the help of runners from the rhizome. Shoots are formed at the tip of the rhizome and the runners which begin to sprout in the autumn are able to survive the winter. Sometimes the lower part of the moss covering can be completely intertwined with rhizomes and runners. Although the Creeping Lady's Tresses can produce its own food, it is thought to be heavily dependent on its fungus partners. Very often its entire underground system is interwoven with the fungus. The Creeping Lady's Tresses grows mainly in mossy pine woods, but it is also found in birch woods. It is never seen in large numbers, and usually grows as a single plant or as scattered clumps. It needs light for flowering and therefore benefits from forest thinning and moderate clearance, but it shuns more heavily cultivated ground.

The genus *Goodyera* has about a hundred species which are found in forests and woodlands throughout the world. *Goodyera repens* itself has been recorded from most of Europe and in the British Isles. It extends to the temperate zones of Asia and North America as well as North Africa.

fruiting stem

Spiranthes spiralis

(L.) Chevall. (*spiranthes* and *spiralis*: the spiral shape of the inflorescence)

Autumn Lady's Tresses

This species with its inflorescences resembling plaits with flowers stuck onto them, is quite different in appearance from most other European orchids. The genus *Spiranthes* which has only three species in Europe, but many more in North America and elsewhere, is related to *Goodyera* which can sometimes have its flowers arranged in a definite spiral. The Autumn Lady's Tresses has a short rhizome, often with roots swollen into tubers not unlike those of dahlias in shape. The stalk, surrounded by sheath-like leaves, is glandular. At the base there is a rosette of withered leaves, and beside it the start of the new green rosette which grows during the late autumn and winter. The flowers, arranged in a tight spiral, are white to green-white and shaped like a bell. The broad lip, which resembles a scoop, has two nectar glands at the base and almost entirely surrounds the column. The forward part is flat and wrinkled and acts as a landing stage for visiting bees and bumble-bees. The pollinia, shaped like a leaf, are fastened to a small disc which is part of the rostellum. Newly-opened flowers have a narrow opening into which the insect inserts its proboscis or other mouth parts. The lower part of the rostellum splits and the sticky disc carrying the pollinia attaches itself to the insect when it leaves the flower. When insects visit another inflorescence, parts of the fragile pollinia can be left in the older flowers lower down. These have a bigger opening and accessible stigmas because the rostellum has shrivelled. When the insect crawls up the spike, it enters younger flowers; in this way it again covers itself in pollen.

The Autumn Lady's Tresses is fairly common, especially in chalk and limestone grasslands and near the sea. Unlike most European orchids it can be invasive, usually into fallow fields and previously disturbed downland. It can also appear on grass lawns and tennis courts but flowers only when these are not regularly mown. Flowers as a rule come late, towards the end of the summer and in the autumn, but the numbers vary greatly from year to year. Because plantlets can develop on the stem, the plant will propagate itself without flowering.

Spiranthes spiralis occurs throughout Europe as far north as Denmark, southwards to North Africa and eastwards to Turkey. In the British Isles it is quite widespread in England, Wales and Eire but has not yet been reported from Scotland. The ploughing of many chalk downlands during the last fifty years has reduced the number of locations where it once grew.

Spiranthes romanzoffiana

Cham. (*romanzoffiana*: after a Russian patron, Count Romanoff)

Irish Lady's Tresses

There are only three species of *Spiranthes* found in Europe but many occur in North America and one species, *Spiranthes sinensis* (Pers.) Ames, is found throughout tropical Asia, Australasia and in orchid houses all over the world. The most interesting species found in Europe is *S. romanzoffiana* which grows in Ireland, in a few places in western Scotland and on Dartmoor in southwest England. Outside of the British Isles it extends across parts of Asia and large parts of the North American continent to Kamchatka and the Aleutians, but it is not known elsewhere in Europe.

S. aestivalis

The flowers are arranged in three spirally-curved rows on a hairy glandular stem which carries the leaves at its base. The white to cream yellow and somewhat tubular or bell-shaped flowers open in July or the beginning of August. The structure and conditions for pollination of the *Spiranthes* flowers have already been described (see p. 54). Pollination of this species is carried out by bumble-bees and bees, but detailed investigation of the European populations are incomplete.

In North America, this orchid can grow to about 50 cm in height, but in Europe it is generally shorter. The plant grows in boggy and other peaty habitats and also in fields and meadows with a high water-table.

Spiranthes aestivalis

(Poir.) Rich. (from Latin *aestivalis*: belonging to the summer)

Summer Lady's Tresses

In England and other places in northern Europe where it once grew, the Summer Lady's Tresses now appears to be extinct. It has also been recorded in many other parts of Europe, extending to North Africa and Turkey, but in most of these sites it is now disappearing so fast that it may become completely extinct before the end of the century. The Summer Lady's Tresses is a plant of damp, acid-soil areas – it is drainage and other agricultural improvement schemes that are leading to its demise. It appears to be relatively safe only in southern Europe where it grows on mountainsides up to 1500 m above sea-level. *Spiranthes aestivalis* is similar to *S. spiralis* but the flowers are longer, narrower, a purer white and more spaced out along the stem. Like other species it has a pleasant scent which becomes stronger in the evening. Moths have been suggested as pollinators but no thorough investigations seem to have been made.

56–57

Malaxis paludosa

(L.) Sw. (*malakos*: soft, tender, *paludosa*: grows in marshland)

Bog Orchid

One must search for a long time before finding this inconspicuous yellow-green orchid, which often merges with
other vegetation and the clumps of bog mosses in which it
grows. The Bog Orchid is very small and slender, not more
than 8–10 cm tall. The underground parts consist basically
of two tubers surrounded by leaf sheaths, arranged one above
the other. One of these belongs to the previous year's growth.
In the bog moss, the nodes of the rhizome are elongated and
the tubers are widely separated from each other and from the
flowering shoot. The roots are hair-like, and for its food
supply the plant is almost entirely dependent on its fungus
partner. The yellowish-green leaves are few, oval and very
fleshy. The tight inflorescence is also a light yellow-green, and
often accounts for more than half the height of the plant. The
flowers are very small but most unusual. Their long stem is
twisted a full 360°, which means that the lip becomes directed
upwards. There are only two other orchids that twist in the
same way, *Malaxis monophyllos* and *Liparis loeselii*. In all of
our other species the flowers are turned through 180° and the
lip is directed downwards. The Bog Orchid lip has a hollow in
the shape of a bowl, but otherwise resembles the other petals.
Flowers appear at the height of the summer and in early
autumn. There is very little information on the pollination
processes of the Bog Orchid but it is probable that it is pollinated by small insects such as flies and midges. It is quite
common to see the erect, small, ripe seed pods indicating that
pollination and fruiting have taken place. The seeds float on
the water, which is how the plant spreads. Another peculiarity
of *Malaxis paludosa* is that it does not entirely depend on
seed formation for its survival. Each leaf has a large number
of small buds on its outer extremity which can be released
to form new plants.

Malaxis paludosa, which in some books is referred to as
Hammarbya paludosa (L.) O. Kuntze, is one of the few of our
orchids which can survive in a really acidic environment. It
is found almost exclusively among very wet sphagnum moss
in bogs and fens, where it often accompanies other well-
known bog plants such as sundew. It occurs throughout the
British Isles but is nowhere very common, partly because its
habitat is rare and also because it is so often overlooked. The
Bog Orchid has been reported from all parts of Europe,
temperate Asia and North America. Outside of Europe the
genus *Malaxis* has over 300 species spread over nearly every
country except New Zealand and Antarctica.

plantlet buds
on leaves

Malaxis monophyllos

(L.) Sw.   (*malakos*: soft, tender, *monophyllos*: with one leaf)

Single-leaved Bog Orchid

alder

This rare, graceful orchid is so well hidden in the dense growth of lime-rich alder carr that luckily it is often unnoticed. These typical sites can be easily damaged by too much walking on, and, unfortunately, it is not unusual to see small bogs and ditches trampled by people searching for orchids. One should always be very careful when wandering in these habitats.

As the Latin name *Malaxis monophyllos* implies, this plant generally carries one leaf, usually oval or spear-shaped. However, at the base there are two additional sheath-like leaves surrounding the stalk. The underground part of the plant consists of two tubers placed very close together. It is from one of these that the fragile slender stalk emerges, which is the growth for the year. The older tubers very often remain, and one can sometimes see three or four together, as in the illustration. The plant grows to a height of 10–25 cm. The small pale yellow-green flowers form a narrow, elongated and lax inflorescence; just as with the ordinary Bog Orchid, they are rotated through a whole circle, and thus have a lip which points upwards. The narrow petal and sepals are spread out and give the flower the appearance of an insect or a spider, which accounts for its Continental name of Gnat Flower. Very little is known about the pollination process; it is possible that small insects carry out some pollination, but self-fruiting can also take place.

The Single-leaved Bog Orchid comes into flower during June and July. It is found in various fens and calcareous swamps and wet ground in woods and scrubland, but it seems to do best in alder carr. Its leaves are hard to find among the leaves of other plants such as Marsh Violets which also grow in these habitats, and it is difficult to judge how far the species extends in Europe. It can easily be missed even by a trained field botanist and sometimes it has disappeared from some of its sites because of draining and disturbance by forest clearance. Also, it seems that it does not flower regularly. It is known to occur in a belt across central Sweden and in the south-eastern parts of Norway and Finland, but it is not found in Denmark or Iceland. Outside of Scandinavia this orchid occurs over large parts of central Europe extending eastwards through Russia to northeast Asia and Alaska. In North America *Malaxis monophyllos* is replaced by its close relative sub-species *brachypoda* (A. Gray) Morris & Eames, but many botanists regard the American plant as no more than a variety of the European species.

stem tubers

Liparis loeselii

(L.) L. C. Rich. (from *liparos*: fatty, bright [leaves] and *loeselii*: after J. Loesel, seventeenth-century German botanist)

Fen Orchid

The Fen Orchid is a rare plant found not only in fens but also in the damp slacks of sand dunes. Its relatives are mainly tropical, many of them gaudy epiphytes living in the tops of trees in the jungle, but there are also several other temperate species in North America, China and Japan. Just as with the ordinary and the Single-leaved Bog Orchid and their tropical relations, the Fen Orchid has a swollen base to the stem which serves as a food store for the growing shoot. As a rule both this year's and last year's tubers are found at the bottom of each flowering shoot, as shown in the illustration. In deep moss, the tubers look like beads in a necklace.

The plant seems to be able to provide itself with nourishment through normal roots and does not need fungus partners. The stem, which is generally short, is surrounded by two almost erect, tongue-shaped, shiny leaves. In the form found in dune-slacks the leaves are broader and blunter and the plants are distinguished as variety *ovata*. Below the leaves there are short sheaths. There are only a few small, pale, yellow-green flowers. The petals, which remain after the fruit has set, are narrow and spread out. The lip, directed upwards as the result of making a complete turn, is broader and bright green at the base. The Fen Orchid flowers towards the end of June and in July. Although very little is known about the pollination mechanism, it is thought that it is self-pollinating. In *Liparis* and closely-related genera, the stamen is shaped like a lid or the peak of a cap. In the Fen Orchid it leans far forward on the stalk, and thus easily drops off. The pollinia easily slide out and attach themselves to the stigma. The rather large seed pods only burst open when the walls have decayed. The orchid also propagates itself by producing root tubers at the base of the plant.

The permanently wet fens and slacks where the Fen Orchid is generally found are increasingly threatened by drainage, and many of its former sites are now extensively ditched. Very often the plant seems to be resourceful, apparently vanishing from one of its sites, only to reappear and flower several years later.

Liparis loeselii occurs over wide areas of Europe but does not extend to the Mediterranean region or further north than southern Sweden and Norway. It is also found in the eastern United States and Canada. In Hawaii *Liparis hawaiensis* H. Mann. is somewhat similar, although considerably more robust. In the British Isles the Fen Orchid is still found in Norfolk and the variety *ovata*, previously known only from southern Wales sand dunes, has recently been seen in the dunes of north Devon.

62–63

Corallorhiza trifida

Chatel. (*corallorhiza*: coral root, *trifida*: in three parts)

Coral Root

Coral Root is saprophytic. It is very unassuming, but its pale slender stalk and delicate inflorescence make it stand out against the darkness of the alder marsh or fungus timber. Although it does contain some chlorophyll and is greener than many other saprophytes, it is almost entirely dependent on the fungus interwoven in its underground system. This system is a coral-like, branched, whitish ground stem with short branches. It has wart-like buds with short tufts of hair. It depends to a large extent on these tufts of hair for its food, obtained by means of fungus threads in the hairs. Several stalks, generally 10–13 cm high, can grow from the ground stem. The stalk is surrounded by leaf sheaths, and is unusually tall in comparison to the very short sparse flower cluster. The small flowers, with triangular supporting leaves, vary from white-yellow to green-yellow. Three of the petals are bent together and two are extended like the wings of a bird in flight. The bent lip is white with red stripes and has a channel in the middle. As far as we know the faintly scented flowers do not have any nectar, so it is not established that the small flies and beetles which visit the flowers really help in pollination. It seems, instead, that there is self-pollination. Coral Root flowers in the early summer. The green ripe seed pods are large and oval and hang down. Seed production seems to be very efficient, which is important because Coral Root apparently does not have an effective way of propagating and spreading by means of its underground system. One often sees the characteristic fruit formation still in position in the year after flowering.

Coral Root does best in damp shaded woods and on heaths and the edges of marshland. It is also found in more open country in sandy soil and in damp places where there is sand; it does not seem to depend on chalk.

Coral Root is confined mostly to the north, around the Arctic and over the whole northern hemisphere. About a dozen closely-related plants grow in North America. Like other northern orchids, its more southern sites are principally on mountains and at considerable heights.

fruiting stem

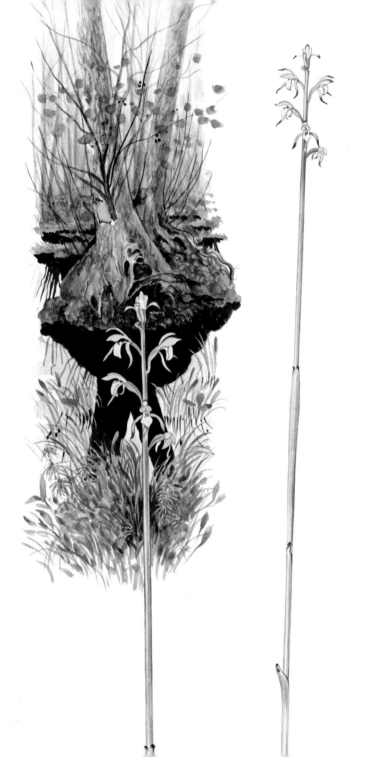

Calypso bulbosa

(L.) Oakes (*Kalypso*: a sea-nymph in mythology, *bulbosa*: with tuber)

Calypso

The species acquired its Latin name from Kalypso, daughter of Atlas, the beautiful nymph who kept the shipwrecked hero Ulysses on her island for seven years. This treasure in the pine woods of Scandinavia, Russia and North America – far distant from its tropical relatives – has been an object of attention and the centre of romantic myths.

Calypso bulbosa has a short, tightly-branching rhizome. The entire short stalk emerges from a tuber surrounded by a sheath-like leaf. Next to this tuber, the growth for the year, there are one or two older ones. A single broad, oval, dark-green leaf, with nerves on the upper side and purple on the lower side, shoots from the ground tuber. There are brownish leaf sheaths and the flower's pink subtending bract on the stalk. The large pink flowers are solitary. The front of the lip is pale and flat and the rear part, with brown streaks, is indented and extended to make a double spur. There are yellow tufts of hair at the entrance. The narrow perianth is pink to reddish violet. The flowers have a vanilla scent but no nectar, yet they are visited and pollinated by female bumble-bees. The flower is well adapted to its pollinators: the pollinia are protected by a hood and the rostellum prevents contact between the male and female organs. A visiting bumble-bee must crawl deep inside the flower to reach the spurs. When the bee withdraws, the pollinia attach themselves to a particular spot on the insect's back. Only if it has the pollinia on its back can the insect penetrate the stigma cavity when visiting another flower. The blueberry flowers, which bloom at the same time as the Calypso, allow the bee to feed on their nectar. This is one of the reasons why Calypso exists in northern climates.

The Calypso grows in damp mossy woods, generally beside rotting tree stumps. It is found in Sweden and Finland and extends to northern Russia and Asia. There is uncertainty as to whether or not the North American Calypso is a separate species or merely a geographical variation of the Eurasian plant. There have been records of *Calypso bulbosa* being found growing wild in various parts of Great Britain but none of these have been substantiated. However, it grows well in very cool alpine greenhouses and may have occurred in Scottish pine woods in the past.

spur

Platanthera bifolia

(L.) Rchb. (*platos*: broad, *anthera*: anther, *bifolia*: two-leaved)

Lesser Butterfly Orchid

This graceful white ornament with its carnation scent at dusk, and root tubers reputed to have medical properties which give strength, is the most generally known, described and, not unnaturally, the most gathered of all our orchids. It is one of our commoner species growing in fields, and belongs to a group of orchids with undivided root tubers and wide leaves. Its two oval root tubers are drawn out to an extended point.

The flowering stem, up to a height of 45 cm, grows from the tubers which in the previous year stored food. At its base are a pair of large tongue-shaped leaves with smaller narrower leaves higher up. The large inflorescence has many widely-separated white or yellow-white rather straggly flowers. The narrow lip of even width has a long, narrow, crooked spur rich in nectar. The sides of the column are placed so that the two anther sacs are parallel. There is a sticky disc beneath each sac. The Lesser Butterfly Orchid flowers in June and July. Its scent becomes stronger in the evening, and attracts moths, mostly hawk moths, and flies which collect nectar from the deep spurs. When the insect arrives, the sticky discs fasten themselves to the base of its long proboscis and the pollinia are dragged out. The pollinium then sways with the club end forward and easily attaches itself to the stigma of the next flower visited.

The Lesser Butterfly Orchid grows in varied surroundings – woods rich in ground cover, fields, heathland, road and rail verges, marshland and the sides of ditches. However, on account of changes in the type and extent of agricultural operations and techniques such as drainage and land improvement it has lately become less common here. It occurs throughout Europe, much of temperate northern and central Asia and extends southwards to North Africa.

fruiting stem

Platanthera chlorantha

(Custer) Rchb.   (*chlorantha*: with green flowers)

Greater Butterfly Orchid

Most non-botanists are hardly aware that in Britain we have
two closely-related species of Butterfly Orchid. The strong,
tall, greenish Greater Butterfly Orchid with a very delicate
smell and green-white flowers sometimes grows together with
the Lesser Butterfly Orchid. When the two flower types are
closely compared one finds that the anther sacs, which in
the Lesser Butterfly Orchid are parallel and lie close together,
are widely separated in the Greater Butterfly Orchid and
converge upwards in the shape of an inverted horseshoe.
The wide cylindrical cluster of flowers has several widely
separated blooms. Pollination takes place in more or less the
same way as in the Lesser Butterfly Orchid. The insect catches
the sticky discs and the pollinia on its protruding eyes.
Whether or not the flowers of *Platanthera chlorantha* are
normally scented has been the subject of much debate. There
are instances recorded, and there seems no reason to doubt
them, of both scented and unscented specimens growing in the
same colony. It is clear that further investigations are required
into both types and possible hybrids between them, and this
work could be done where both grow together.

It seems that the Greater Butterfly Orchid is more
dependent on shade and a calcareous soil than the Lesser
Butterfly Orchid. It grows mainly in downland and scrubby
and wooded situations. Formerly it was rarer than the
P. bifolia, but this now seems to be the reverse in many places
throughout Europe. The Greater Butterfly Orchid likes wild
ground where shrubs are beginning to grow. Because its root
system is strongly intertwined with its fungus partners, food
supplies are assured even in very shaded ground where there
is plenty of decay. Flowering occurs later than with the Lesser
Butterfly, but both species can be found in flower between
mid-June and early August. The fruiting stem is very characteristic, with closely packed and erect oval seed capsules.

Throughout Asia and Europe the Greater Butterfly Orchid
has more or less the same general distribution as the Lesser
Butterfly Orchid but it is not quite so commonly en-
countered at higher altitudes and seems to prefer the slightly
warmer and drier zones. It occurs throughout the British
Isles. There are many species of *Platanthera* found in North
America: formerly all were included in the large genus
Habenaria but this is now redefined to include only the
species found in the tropical regions of South America,
Africa, Asia and the Pacific islands.

fruiting stem

P. bifolia

P. chlorantha

70–71

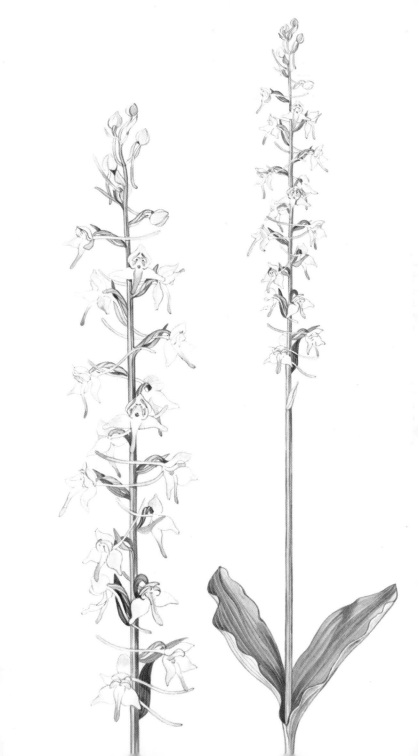

Platanthera obtusata ssp. *oligantha*

(Turcz.) Hult. (*obtusatus*: blunt [leaves], *oligo*: few, *anthos*: flower)

Lapp Orchid

We only come across the Lapp Orchid, the rarest orchid in northern Europe, in special habitats in Norway and Sweden where it grows along with dwarf 'Arctic' willows, the Alpine Butterwort and other rare mountain species. It is barely 10 cm tall, with a short inflorescence and only a few unscented flowers. Below the flowers, the stalk has a narrow upright leaf and a large oval leaf at the base. The perianth is whitish yellow with green markings. The narrow lip is shaped like a tongue and has a short spur. It is possible that the plants are pollinated by flies. Because the Lapp Orchid only flowers sporadically and can only be found high in the mountains, it is often overlooked. In Sweden it grows only in and near the Abisko National Park, on the slopes of Mount Nuolja and in the Torne marshes immediately beneath. The other known occurrences, about ten altogether, are in northern Norway. The related sub-species *obtusata*, often confused with the Lapp Orchid, is found widely over stretches of North America and in some parts of northern Asia.

Platanthera hyperborea

(L.) Lindl. (*hyperborea*: extreme north, most northerly)

Arctic Orchid

The Greenland or Arctic Orchid, the fourth species of Butterfly Orchid in Europe, does not occur in the British Isles but grows fairly commonly in the open spaces of Iceland. It is fairly tall and robust with many flowers tightly packed together. The base of the stalk is surrounded by a short broad leaf which resembles a trumpet. The other leaves are broad and spear-shaped and spread along the stalk. At the top they become the bract subtending the whole inflorescence. Some reports say that the yellow-green flowers have no scent, others say they have a pleasant one. The lip and spur are longer than in the Lapp Orchid. It is probable that the flowers are self-pollinating. The Arctic Orchid is widely distributed in the northern part of Iceland and it grows in a variety of different types of open country, heaths and moorlands. Outside Iceland it is found, as its alternative name suggests, in Greenland as well as in eastern Asia and North America. The only known European occurrences of the Lapp Orchid and the Arctic Orchid are in Scandinavia.

P. obtusata ssp. *oligantha*   *P. hyperborea*

Coeloglossum viride

(L.) Hartm. (*koilos*: hollow, *glossa*: tongue, *viride*: green)

Frog Orchid

It is not easy to find the Frog Orchid in the grassy banks and open scrubland where it grows, and it is often trampled. It has no bright colours to contrast with the surrounding vegetation, and on first sight it seems to be quite unimportant. At the stalk base there are two large, blunt-ended elliptical leaves, and higher up there are two narrow, pointed ones. The underground system is dominated by deeply rooted tubers. The green to green-yellow inflorescence has irregularly twisted flowers and some sprawling supporting leaves. The faint-smelling flowers have a long, extended, hanging, blunted three-pointed lip. The sepals and petals form a cap or helmet over the lip. The spur is short. Flowers appear during most of the summer and are visited by small insects. The sticky discs at the mouth of the spur fasten the pollinia onto the insect's head. They are inclined slightly forward and easily come in contact with the stigma of the next flower visited. It seems that pollination is efficient because the seeds set fairly early and in considerable quantity.

This orchid can be found in both deciduous and coniferous woods as well as rough pastures and grassy banks. It prefers calcareous soils but is not confined to them. In mountainous areas it is found above the tree level on open moorland. In Asia, it occurs up to 4000 m above sea-level. The northern plants are usually darker in colour and the mountain forms of Frog Orchid are very often stunted with stalks and flowers of strong red, purple or brown shades. In North America the Frog Orchid has extra-long bracts and is often distinguished as a separate sub-species var. *virescens* (Muhl.) Luer. The Frog Orchid forms hybrids with a number of species from other genera such as *Orchis*, *Dactylorhiza* and *Gymnadenia* and these are quite frequently reported from various parts of the British Isles.

Coeloglossum viride occurs throughout central and northern Europe as well as Asia and in North America. In southern Europe it is confined to the mountainous regions but in the British Isles it has been found in almost every county, although because of changes to its habitat it is now more common in the north and west.

mountain form

Pseudorchis albida

(L.) A. & D. Löve (*pseudo*: false, *orchis*: orchid, *albida*: white)

Small White Orchid

In the British Isles *Pseudorchis albida* is not at all common but nevertheless it has been given several 'common' names such as the Small White Orchid, Small White Mountain Orchid, White Fragrant Orchid and White Frog Orchid. Similarly, in Scandinavia it has been called the White Ox, Hammer Spur and White Bridal Spur. This diminutive orchid has even gathered several Latin names, including *Leucorchis albida*, *Habenaria albida* and *Gymnadenia albida*.

The underground part of the Small White Orchid consists of deep indented root tubers and horizontal roots usually interwoven with fungus threads. The very short stalk with its widely-spaced leaves has a dense cylindrical inflorescence. The spice-scented flowers are generally dirty white or pale yellow, sometimes with a green streak. They are bell-shaped and hang on one side. The trilobed lip has a hammer-shaped spur with nectar. In var. *straminea* (the plant found in the mountains of northern Europe) it is shaped like a pouch, but in var. *albida* (the type found in the rest of Europe) it is the same thickness throughout. It seems that bees and butter-flies and even other insects are attracted by the scent of the flowers. Pollination seems to be carried out in the same way as in its near relations the Frog and Butterfly Orchids. There is also self-pollination in the older flowers in which the pollinia drop onto the stigma. The Small White Orchid forms natural hybrids with species from several other related genera: these include × *Pseudinium* (Small White × Musk Orchid), × *Pseudadenia* (Small White × Fragrant Orchid) and × *Pseudorhiza* (Small White × Spotted Orchid).

The Small White Orchid is found throughout Europe but is nowhere very common and it seems to be disappearing from many of its former localities. It is basically a plant of pastures and moorland but is not very particular as to the type of soil it prefers. The disturbance by land improvement schemes has led to its reduced numbers but paradoxically the discontinuance of grazing can also lead to its local extinction. In the British Isles it is virtually confined to the higher ground (150 m or more above sea-level) of northern England, Scotland, Wales and Ireland. Outside of Europe *P. albida* is widespread, and has been recorded from tem-perate Asia, North America and Greenland.

Nigritella nigra

(L.) Rchb.   (*nigra*: black)

Black Vanilla Orchid

Although it is not one of the larger orchids, this striking mountain plant has a singular beauty. In the Alps it vies with the Edelweiss for attention, and has been given countless names. The deep purple to black-red, almost spherical inflorescence shows up clearly against the green vegetation of open fields. At the bottom of the angular robust stalk there are tightly-packed leaves resembling spears at regular intervals, and higher up there are shorter, stiff and erect leaves. The root tubers are deeply divided. The tightly-grouped flowers have long supporting leaves. Because the ovary is not twisted, the lip is directed upwards: it has roughly the same shape as other perianths but it is somewhat wider and has a sac-like spur. The star-shaped spread-out perianth tends to make the flowers less orchid-like. The strongly-coloured flowers which are used, among other things, to colour brandy, have a pronounced vanilla scent. Little is known of the biology of its pollination, but it is said that butterflies are constant visitors, and it is thought they are probably also pollinators. Flowering takes place in early and high summer.

To see the plant's flowers *en masse* one must visit the mountains and alpine regions of the Continent. It still grows in large quantities on the rich alpine fields, far from any roads, sometimes to heights of over 2000 m. In Sweden it grows in lower-lying ground. It does well in dry calcareous meadows and fields, especially on the hills. Occasionally it appears in sub-alpine open shrubland.

There is also an eastern alpine form, *Nigritella miniata* or *N. rubra*, which is sometimes regarded as a separate species but it is uncertain as to whether the two types really are botanically distinct. Like several of its relatives *Nigritella nigra* can be promiscuous and several hybrids have been recorded between it and species of other genera. These include × *Dactylitella* (*Nigritella* × *Dactylorhiza*), × *Nigrorchis* (*Nigritella* × *Orchis*) and × *Pseuditella* (*Nigritella* × *Pseudorchis*).

The Brown Woman, as the Black Vanilla Orchid has been called in Scandinavia, which used to be common in hay fields and meadows in the region, has recently become rarer. In order to protect the species a conservation programme 'Action Brown Woman' has been started, supported by the World Wildlife Fund.

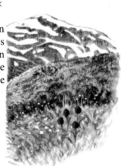

Gymnadenia conopsea

(L.) R. Br.   (*gymnos*: exposed, *aden*: gland, *konos*: fly, *opsis*: appearance)

Fragrant Orchid

A field where Fragrant Orchid grows can look as if it has been painted pink and pale violet. One can still find several places where this elegant orchid grows in abundance and although in some places it is becoming scarce, the Fragrant Orchid is fairly common. Sometimes it grows to a height of about 45 cm. At the stalk base there are some long ribbon-like leaves. The root tubers divide into two indented lobes.

The Fragrant Orchid flowers in June and often retains its flowers until long past midsummer. The colour can vary from pure white to pink, pale red-violet and reddish purple. The lip is broad and trilobed and the long spur is almost thread-like and filled with nectar. The flower's fragrance is spice with a hint of carnation. The scent becomes stronger in the evening and attracts both butterflies and moths. Insects with long tongues looking for nectar come in contact with the narrow, exposed sticky discs and drag the pollinia with them on their way out of the flower. The pollinia protrude here as well, and their loose package of pollen is then easily attached to the stigma of another flower (see p. 15).

var. *densiflora*

As the Fragrant Orchid varies a great deal in colour, appearance and size, many forms and species have been described. In several parts of England and Wales a more robust, darker and later-flowering type with wide leaves (as seen in the illustration) grows on wetter ground. This form, called var. *densiflora* (Wahlenb.) Lindl., has a very marked clove scent in its tightly-packed flowers and it has been recorded up to a metre in height. In certain islands of the Outer Hebrides a much smaller and dull reddish-purple flowered form. var. *insulicola* H. Harr., has been found. It is further distinguished by the unpleasant rubber-like smell of its flowers.

Even if many hay fields have now disappeared and intensive cultivation or re-use of land has altered the habitats of the Fragrant Orchid, it is still found fairly widely over the whole of the British Isles on open land and in chalk pits. It is not found in woodland. The total distribution of the Fragrant Orchid extends throughout Eurasia southwards to Iran and the Mediterranean. It has crossed quite commonly with species from other genera to give many bigeneric hybrids such as × *Dactylogymnadenia* (Fragrant × Marsh or Spotted Orchids), × *Gymnaglossum* (Fragrant × Frog Orchids), × *Gymnanacamptis* (Fragrant × Pyramidal Orchids), × *Gymnaplatanthera* (Fragrant × Butterfly Orchids), × *Gymnigritella* (Fragrant × Black Vanilla Orchids), × *Gymnotraunsteinera* (*Gymnadenia* × *Traunsteinera*) and × *Pseudadenia* (Fragrant × Small White Orchids).

Gymnadenia odoratissima

(L.) L. C. Rich. (*odoratissima*: highly scented)

Short-spurred Fragrant Orchid

The Short-spurred Fragrant Orchid belongs to the rarities in
the European flora. The common and Latin names indicate
that it is particularly strongly or pleasantly scented, but one
must generally be sceptical when it comes to exaggerated
descriptions of smells. Many who have compared *Gymnadenia odoratissima* with *G. conopsea* report that the scents
vary or are non-existent. It has been said that the Short-
spurred Fragrant Orchid has a stronger scent than the
Fragrant Orchid during the daytime. This orchid is very
similar to the Fragrant Orchid, but is generally smaller in
every way. The slender stalk has very narrow, long ribbon-
like leaves at its base, and like the ordinary Fragrant Orchid
there are some short leaves higher up. The inflorescence is
generally narrow and the flowers are usually pale red-violet.
There are, however, some purple-red, white or yellow-white
forms, the latter called variety *ochroleuca*. The flowers differ
in several small details from *Gymnadenia conopsea*, mainly
in the much shorter spur, about the length of the fruit-body.
The lip is more deeply grooved. Very little information is
available on the pollination procedure of the Short-spurred
Fragrant Orchid. The plant blooms at the same time as later-
flowering specimens of *G. conopsea*.

Gymnadenia odoratissima has not yet been reliably recorded in the British Isles. Several reports have been made
from localities in many parts of England and the Scottish
islands but there is no convincing evidence that it should have
been considered as a member of the British flora now extinct.
It is confined to Europe and is rarely very common, but on
the island of Gotland, in the Baltic Sea, it can be seen in some
quantity in favourable years. The Short-spurred Fragrant
Orchid is found especially in lime-rich marshes and fens but
it also occurs in more acid bogs and other places that are
flooded in winter and spring. In Russia it occurs in coniferous
woods, especially in the more open parts and clearings, but
drainage and other operations pose a threat to its survival.

Neottianthe cucullata (L.) Schltr. (*neottianthe*: with flowers
like *Neottia, cucullata*: with hood or cowl) is a European/
Asiatic species which occurs in large areas of Russia, Japan
and China. It is occasionally found in Poland and the Baltic
regions.

The flowers are arranged on one side of the stem which
has two wide leaves at the base. The perianth is pointed and
drawn to a hood or cone. The species grows in damp coniferous and mixed forests and flowers late in the summer.

Neottianthe cucullata

Dactylorhiza sambucina

(L.) Soó   (*daktylos*: finger, *rhiza*: root, *sumbucina*: similar to *Sambucus* [elder, has a similar scent to the elder])

Elder-flowered Orchid

Which is Adam and which is Eve? This question concerning a popular European name (Adam and Eve) for this species is often asked by amateur botanists when they first see the two differently-coloured forms of this orchid. The root tubers, at one time the object of peasant superstitions, may be another reason for the name; they resemble human bodies pressed together, one pale (the current year's) and the other dark (last year's). The indented root tubers (in this species substantially divided in half) is one reason why a number of orchids have been separated from the relatively large genus *Orchis* and formed into their own genus *Dactylorhiza* (see pp. 100, 104). The colour forms and their interesting separation and distribution are a series of genetic-ecological problems for which no solution has yet been found. However, in the literature the yellow-white form is considered typical: it is often the only one to be found. In Norway it is the only one, and on the Baltic island of Gotland and on the Continent it is more common than the purple-red one.

The flowers are arranged in a compact spike with long supporting leaves. The broad lip is roughly the shape of a cloverleaf, while the spur is long and strong. The lip has red-violet spots in the yellow form, and yellow shading in the red form. The flowers do not last long, and the plant quickly withers. The scent recalls that of an elder-tree flower. Many species of *Orchis*, *Dactylorhiza* and their close relatives have a similarly highly-developed mechanism for pollination (see p. 14). The Elder-flowered Orchid does not occur in the British Isles but is frequently found on the Continent, flowering as early as May, scattered around hills and stony ground, giving them a reddish hue with a splash of yellow. Sometimes the normally stunted but robust plants form colourful groupings with intermediate forms of different shades of yellow-red. According to investigations carried out on Gotland, it seems that the red form is usually confined to the coast. *Dactylorhiza sambucina* is one of the orchids very dependent on, and encouraged by, the effects of civilization: walking, grazing and land reclaiming. It does well in dry ground with stunted grass, but it also appears in open deciduous woodland.

In Sweden the species is common in large areas of the east coast, especially around Stockholm, and in other places in Scandinavia. Its distribution is otherwise largely limited to central and southern Europe where it is essentially a mountain plant. There the red form is rare.

Dactylorhiza incarnata

(L.) Soó (*incarnata*: the colour of meat)

Early Marsh Orchid

The Early Marsh Orchid is really a collective name for a large number of shapes, varieties, hybrids and ecological types grouped together as the species *D. incarnata*. Many of the forms result from the numerous hybrids within the species and with other species, as well as from variation resulting from the effects of the environment. On this and the following pages we describe the more commonly-occurring plants within the Early Marsh Orchid aggregate, some of them as sub-species even if they should really be considered as separate species or varieties or, possibly, not be considered as worthy of any nomenclatural distinction.

The whole complex of these orchids is characterized by erect, mainly unmarked leaves with a markedly hooded apex; a robust, straight and somewhat hollow stalk and a cylindrical inflorescence with prominent bracts. It is not easy even for anyone fully acquainted with orchids to discover in the wild an unequivocal representative of the original of *Dactylorhiza incarnata* (ssp. *incarnata*). This typical sub-species is an average-sized orchid with narrow, unmarked, spear-shaped leaves. The flower axis is very small and narrow, and the bracts are about the same length as the flower. The flowers are flesh-pink (rarely pale red-violet) but there are also some albino forms (ssp. *incarnata* var. "*alba*"). The slightly furrowed lip has darker-coloured loop markings. The spur is bent downwards.

fruiting stem

The Early Marsh Orchid occurs more plentifully in calcareous soils, but the plant is not confined to this type of habitat. It does well on damp ground, in wet meadows, fens, marshes and by the sea. It is also found in more developed ground. The aggregate species is found over large areas of Europe as well as southwestern Asia, and is common throughout the British Isles. The typical sub-species *incarnata* is the commonest type in Great Britain and Ireland but it is disappearing in many localities because of drainage.

A large broad-leaf type with a congested inflorescence and long supporting leaves has been called var. "*latissima*" but many botanists consider it to be a local ecologically-determined modification.

86–87

Dactylorhiza incarnata ssp. *ochroleuca*

(Boll.) P. F. Hunt & Summerh.   (*okros*: pale, *leukos*: white)

White or Fen Early Marsh Orchid

The orchid seeker will find a carpet of every shade of red and violet in calcareous fens in East Anglia and southern Wales. Sometimes the red shades are broken by splashes of white. The bone-white or yellow-white orchids stand out like wax candles, almost glowing when dusk falls.

These are not an albino form (*D. incarnata* ssp. *incarnata* var. "*alba*"): that is very rare. These tall yellow-white orchids, with their tightly-packed flowers, have been referred to as sub-species *ochroleuca*, one of the more easily recognizable variations of *D. incarnata*. Sometimes they have been referred to as a separate species. How great a systematic significance should be attributed to orchid colour is a matter open to debate. Some research workers think that it is a question of sorting out two forms, ssp. *ochroleuca* and white-flowering ssp. *incarnata*. Now and again there occur red types of orchids with streaks of yellow and white, forming transitions to entirely yellow or whitish forms. The usual White Early Marsh Orchid flowers have a bone-white to yellow-white perianth with pronounced yellow tinges on the lip but these are not the only differences from the ordinary Early Marsh Orchid. In particular, ssp. *ochroleuca* has rather larger flowers and broad leaves at the base and is really much more robust.

In the British Isles there are at least four other sub-species of *Dactylorhiza incarnata* widely recognized as distinct. One of these, *D. incarnata* ssp. *cruenta*, is dealt with on p. 90, as it is often considered to be a distinct species (*D. cruenta*). *Dactylorhiza incarnata* ssp. *gemmana* (Pugsl.) Soó is a very robust form, often exceeding 50 cm in height and with six or more leaves. It is found primarily in fens in western Ireland and Norfolk. On the peat moors in many parts of the British Isles we find a plant with rich magenta purple flowers called ssp. *pulchella* (Druce) Soó. In sand dunes and especially in the dune-slacks there is a rich crimson or ruby-red flowered form which is treated as ssp. *coccinea* (Pugsl.) Soó. This latter is also found in similar habitats in other parts of Europe.

Dactylorhiza incarnata ssp. *cruenta*

(Muell.) Sell   (*cruenta*: blooded, splashed with blood)

Bloody Early Marsh Orchid

The Bloody or Flecked Early Marsh Orchid is heavily coloured with brown, red and purple. Sometimes it looks scorched by fire, or as if it had been sprinkled with blood or paint. The dark spots on both sides of the leaves, the upper part of the stalk and the bracts vary in appearance. Sometimes they spread over the whole leaf and sometimes they form circles or heavily-coloured dots. The status of *D. incarnata* ssp. *cruenta* as a distinct species is in dispute, as is the case with other plants within the Early Marsh Orchid complex. Intermediate forms are always being found.

The dark purple-red spotted flowers are arranged in a compact axis. The stalk, which is often stunted and strong, carries closely-placed and comparatively broad leaves. The plant prefers chalk and grows in swamps and on damp fields, generally near the sea-shore, but occurs also in cultivated ground. It is found in the British Isles only in western Ireland where it favours highly calcareous fens. Outside this area it is widespread over the European mainland but it is nowhere very common and is frequently confined to higher altitudes such as the Alps where it grows at heights of up to 2000 m.

A plant similar in appearance and distribution to subspecies *cruenta*, but which is not confined to lime-rich soils, is variety *borealis*. It has the usual unspotted, short and narrow leaves but in all its other parts it is more slender than the sub-species *cruenta*.

The Early Marsh Orchid readily forms hybrids with other species of *Dactylorhiza*, and sometimes large 'hybrid-swarm' colonies occur. The hybrids, which are often tall, can sometimes be fertile, and back-crossing with parent species can happen. These hybrids are even more difficult to classify in the *Dactylorhiza* complex. The commonest hybrid is the one with the Common Spotted Orchid (i.e. *D. incarnata × fuchsii*) and is called *Dactylorhiza × kernerorum* (Soó) Soó. Certain of these hybrid plants are very similar to the species *D. praetermissa*. This sometimes frequently-occurring hybrid formation comes from changes that occur through agricultural developments. New environments have been created where both the parent species may flourish and thus the hybrid can establish itself.

Dactylorhiza praetermissa

(Druce) Soó   (*praetermissa*: overlooked, not mentioned)

Southern Marsh Orchid

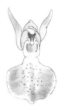

The Southern Marsh Orchid is closely related to the large
group of species, sub-species and hybrids involving the Early
Marsh Orchid *D. incarnata* and outside of the British Isles
it has often been overlooked or included with other similar
types. Some investigators suggest that *Dactylorhiza praetermissa* could very well have been developed as the result of
hybridization between the Early Marsh Orchid and the
Common or Heath Spotted Orchids *Dactylorhiza fuchsii* and
D. maculata.

The Southern Marsh Orchid differs from the Early Marsh
Orchid mainly in its very large flowers with their large
rounded, flat or saucer-shaped lip. The flowers vary from
pale pink-violet to deep red-lilac. The stronger-coloured
flowers are sometimes confused with *D. purpurella* and it can
hybridize with this species. The stem is often taller and
stronger than in the Early Marsh Orchid, and carries several
broad spear-shaped, rather grey-green leaves which are
usually unspotted. The orchid known as *Dactylorhiza "par-
dalina"* is now regarded as being merely a form of *D. praetermissa* with heavily ring-spotted leaves. The specimens with
the brightest, richest magenta flowers are often called var.
pulchella (Druce) Soó.

The Southern Marsh Orchid is found in particular in
marshland rich in lime, but it can also be seen in other types
of wetland where it grows alongside marsh plants such as
sedge rushes and meadowsweet. Sometimes it is found also
in sand dunes or on damp chalky outcrops. The Southern
Marsh Orchid flowers later than the Early Marsh Orchid,
usually from June until the middle of July.

D. praetermissa is quite common in the southern half of
Britain but elsewhere it occurs sporadically. As far as we
know, it is a comparatively rare species, found only in parts
of northern France, Belgium, Holland and Germany. Its
distribution is not fully known, and the same applies to other
forms within the *D. maculata–D. incarnata* complex with
which it is often confused. Sightings have been reported in
Scandinavia, including Norway, but the definite identity of
the plants has not yet been settled to everybody's satisfaction.

Dactylorhiza majalis

(Rchb.) P. F. Hunt & Summerh. (*majalis* from *majus*: the month of May)

Broad-leaved Marsh Orchid

The Broad-leaved Marsh Orchid is found throughout Europe and over much of its range it is fairly consistent in character. However, in several localities, especially at the edge of its distribution, the typical ssp. *majalis* is wholly or partly replaced by other forms. These forms hybridize freely with the 'normal' form to produce a bewildering range of plants, and frequently they cross with other species of *Dactylorhiza* to make the identification and classification an almost impossible task.

The Broad-leaved Marsh Orchid in its typical form is a fairly large plant with red streaks running up its sturdy hollow stalk. Short round leaves are found at the base of the stalk. The lower leaves are fairly wide, large and oval, while the upper ones are shorter, narrower and gradually becoming bracts. The leaves have black-red to purple-red spots on the upper side. The compact head of flowers is rounded or oval. The supporting leaves extend beyond the flowers which are pink to red-purple, with a dark-spotted lip which has two rhombic side lobes and a short central lobe. The short spur is fairly straight.

Dactylorhiza majalis, as its name suggests, flowers at the end of May and the first half of June. It is found in marshes, flooded fields and very damp meadows. It is very sensitive to ditching, draining and similar agricultural upheavals, and recently its numbers have been decimated, but it can still be seen in a number of individual localities. On the Continent it grows both in the mountains, where it is found at heights above 2000 m, and in the lowlands.

In the British Isles *Dactylorhiza majalis* ssp. *majalis* has never been recorded but in Ireland and some of the Scottish islands and one or two localities on the mainland, it is represented by a very closely-related series of plants *D. majalis* ssp. *occidentalis* (Pugsl.) D. A. Webb or, sometimes, *D. kerryensis*. In northern and western Wales, especially on the Isle of Anglesey, another form has been distinguished. This has longer and generally narrower leaves and a different spur to the flowers: it is called *D. majalis* ssp. *cambrensis* (Roberts) Roberts.

Dactylorhiza purpurella

(T. & T. A. Steph.) Soó   (*purpurella*: coloured purple)

Northern Marsh Orchid

The most widespread marsh orchid in the British Isles is the
Early Marsh Orchid *Dactylorhiza incarnata*. However, in the
south and east of England and Wales the commonest species
is the Southern Marsh Orchid *D. praetermissa* and in the
north and west and especially in Scotland we find that the
Northern Marsh Orchid *D. purpurella* is very abundant. This
species is generally smaller than *D. praetermissa* or *D. majalis*.
The strong, usually hollow stalk carries several fairly tightly
compacted, broad, green leaves bent outwards with a broadly
hooded lip. Frequently there are many small, fine, dark
purple spots near the point of the leaf. The flowers vary from
pale or pinkish red to dark rich purple-red, and are gathered
in a compact strong spike. The lip is broadly diamond-shaped
and has dark irregular lines and spots which are more
pronounced than in *D. majalis*. The spur is quite thick and
strong.

The Northern Marsh Orchid flowers fairly late in the
summer. Little is known of the mechanism of pollination. As
hybrids with other *Dactylorhiza* species, especially the spotted
orchids *D. fuchsii* and *D. maculata*, are common wherever
the plant is found, probably bees and bumble-bees are the
pollinators.

The Northern Marsh Orchid is found usually in wet fields,
fens and marshes and often near the coast among dunes and
sand hills.

This orchid is essentially western European with its distribution concentrated in Ireland, northern England, Wales
and Scotland, but its overall distribution is not fully known.
There was also a substantial colony of the species near
Southampton in southern England. Whether or not it was
transplanted in the marshes there will probably never be
known as it is becoming extinct because of hybridization
with other species of *Dactylorhiza* and because the site is
threatened by drainage for a new motorway. Unreliable
sightings have been reported from the western European
mainland. The Scandinavian occurrences of northern Gotland and western Norway represent its most easterly outposts. Among the northern European flora there are several
examples of the Atlantic species with their main distribution
on the British Isles and the coasts of western Europe, species
which have secured a foothold in the north on the Scandinavian west coast. The most northerly locations of the
Northern Marsh Orchid, apart from those on the west coast
of Norway, are in northern Gotland, among the sand dunes,
and on the Faroe Islands.

fruiting stem

96–97

Dactylorhiza traunsteineri

(Saut.) Soó (*traunsteineri*: after J. Traunsteiner, a Tyrolean chemist)

Narrow-leaved Marsh Orchid

This orchid is not at all common in the British Isles but is found in widely separated populations in fens and marshes in central southern England, East Anglia, Lancashire, north-west Wales and several places in Ireland. The plants included in this species comprise a range of forms, the exact nature of which is far from clear. Some botanists even consider it merely a variation of *Dactylorhiza majalis*. The Narrow-leaved Marsh Orchid shows a very great variation in appearance and in environmental requirements and some colonies very closely resemble other *Dactylorhiza* plants, especially forms of the Broad-leaved Marsh Orchid. Typical examples of the species are, however, easily recognized by the few, narrow, ribbon-like and usually somewhat twisted leaves. These are often strongly spotted on the upper side, but variations occur and the spots can sometimes be missing. Another outstanding feature is the characteristic trilobed lip with its strongly protruding long central lobe. The whole orchid has a more delicate appearance than most other marsh orchids. The root tubers, situated at different levels, have extended, almost thread-like, lobes. The large flowers, arranged in a short, spread-out spike, are clear pale red or pink-purple with darker lip markings. The spur is quite long, thick and blunt.

var. *blyttii*

The Narrow-leaved Marsh Orchid flowers during the latter part of June and in July. As already mentioned, this orchid does best in soft ground, mainly in lime-rich fens along with other typical fen and marsh species, but it can grow also in swamp with standing water among the reeds. Some forms usually considered as distinct varieties do, however, occur in other environments. The north European variety *blyttii* is even found on cultivated ground and mountain slopes. This variety, sometimes called *pseudocordigera*, and sometimes regarded as a distinct species, is stunted. It has shorter, wider and almost oval leaves and dark purple-red flowers.

The distribution of *Dactylorhiza traunsteineri* is not at all certain. It definitely occurs in the British Isles and most of Scandinavia but other records are few and far between. However, recent research has suggested that it is probably fairly widespread over northern and central Europe but has been overlooked or confused with other species or with hybrids between other species, especially those involving the narrower-leaved forms of *D. maculata*. In the British Isles it has been given several common names such as the Wicklow Marsh Orchid and Pugsley's Marsh Orchid (after Pugsley the well-known botanist who was especially concerned with Marsh Orchids), but to most orchid-seekers it is usually called 'traunsteineri' or Traunsteiner's Marsh Orchid.

var. *blytii*

Dactylorhiza maculata

(L.) Soó   (*maculata*: spotted [leaves])

Heath Spotted Orchid

When taking a walk over the moorlands and heaths during
the late spring and summer, we frequently come across a
very common orchid. It has many different common names
in the countries where it is found; for example in Scandinavia
it has been called the Spotted Ox, the Virgin Mary's Hand,
God's Hand and The Hand of Shame. In many cases it
carries this name together with the closely-related species
Dactylorhiza fuchsii, the Common Spotted Orchid. The lay-
man may have difficulty distinguishing between the various
sub-species within the genus *Dactylorhiza* because it is not
easy even for the specialist. A good clue to identification is
that all the species in the genus have lobed or 'fingered' root
tubers, from which the name is derived.

maculata ssp. *maculata*

The Heath Spotted Orchid is easily recognized by its
pointed leaves with blue-green or dull purplish-brown spots.
The lower ones are narrow and shaped like a tongue with
a blunt point. The tall slender stalk carries a tightly packed
cluster of flowers in the shape of a pyramid or oval. The
flowers are from bright rose-pink to pure white and variously
marked. The broad flat lip is trilobed with darker markings
in the form of lines, streaks or spots but is very variable in
its colour and detailed shape. Pollination is carried out
mainly by bees, bumble-bees and flies.

Dactylorhiza maculata occurs throughout Europe and
extends into northern Asia and, recently, there have been
reports of its occurrence in North America. As well as the
floral variations, the leaves of this species have a wide range
of shapes and sizes. The original form, ssp. *maculata* as it is
now called, and was described by the Swedish botanist
Linnaeus, is found over much of northern and central
Europe. However, there are many other forms confined to
relatively small geographical areas. Two examples are the
Scandinavian sub-species *kolaensis* and *islandica* and the
British and Irish *D. maculata* ssp. *ericetorum* (E. F. Linton)
P. F. Hunt & Summerh., often loosely referred to as *D.
"ericetorum"*. This latter is fairly similar to ssp. *maculata* but
has narrower leaves and smaller spurs. On the Isle of Rhum
and certain other adjacent islands, in the 'machair' and other
dune areas, a distinct sub-species [*D. maculata* ssp. *rhoumensis*
(H. Harr. f.) Soó] has been reported. Its chief claim to distinct
status is that its lip markings are consistently much heavier
than in ssp. *ericetorum*.

fuchsii

All forms of *Dactylorhiza maculata* grow in damp heaths,
fields and marshes, generally on acid soils but occasionally
in slightly calcareous fens and meadows. It is found at sea-
level and at all altitudes up to 1000 m.

maculata ssp. *ericetorum*

Dactylorhiza fuchsii

(Druce) Soó   (*fuchsii*: after A. Fuchs, an orchid specialist)

Common Spotted Orchid

In damp open woods, on calcareous and clayey soils, in fens,
marshes, meadows, pastures, downland and even on roadside
and railway verges, one frequently comes across a tall leafy
orchid plant with plenty of flowers. This is the Common
Spotted Orchid, probably our most common wild orchid.
However, throughout the rest of Europe its nature and
characteristic features are not fully understood and it has
been recorded from only relatively few areas. It is vaguely
similar to the Heath Spotted Orchid but is usually much
more robust and with a very markedly equal trilobed lip.
Another characteristic feature is the lower leaves which are
always much shorter, wider and blunter than the upper ones.
The lowest leaf shows this characteristic very clearly, so that
the species can be identified even when not in flower. The
spots on the leaves, if present at all, are solid and not ringed

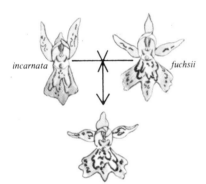

incarnata   fuchsii

hybrid (× *kernerorum*)

and can be coalesced into transverse bars. The spur is much
wider than with *D. maculata* and the lip markings are much
more pronounced – well-defined loops and flecks rather than
fine dots.

Dactylorhiza fuchsii is a variable species and many forms
have been described as distinct varieties or sub-species. These
include sub-species *hebridensis* (Wilmott) Soó and sub-
species *okellyi* (Druce) Soó (from the limestone areas of
northwest Scotland and western Ireland). It hybridizes widely
with other species of *Dactylorhiza* and with those from related
genera.

hybrid

Orchis palustris

Jacq. (*orkhis*: orchid, eg. testicle [indicating root tubers], *palustris*: grows in swamps)

This genus *Orchis* has always attracted botanists and laymen for a great variety of reasons, mainly because of the most unusual flowers of all the species. The botanists have been concerned with the processes of pollination and the classification of this group, with its unending wealth of different floral forms. Eventually it was decided to split the group into two distinct genera, *Orchis* and *Dactylorhiza* (erroneously called *Dactylorchis* for many years). *Orchis* is distinguished by its testiculate root tubers and chaffy bracts and *Dactylorhiza* by its lobed, digitate tubers and leaf-like bracts.

This species, *Orchis palustris*, has lobed tubers and leaf-like bracts. The leaves are few, grass-like and erect. The sparse inflorescence is therefore very prominent, especially as the flowers are unusually large. They are bright purple to red-purple, sometimes paler, and are subtended by purple bracts. The broad lip, with dark spots at the spur opening, hangs straight down. The fairly long thick spur is directed diagonally upwards. It contains no free nectar. The pollination procedure is roughly the same as with most species of the *Orchis* and *Dactylorhiza* (see p. 14). It flowers from the middle of June to the middle of July. Very soon after flowering the plants form new shoots which survive the winter to flower the following year.

Orchis palustris grows best in very swampy ground and consequently has a very loose root system. It has naturally suffered through drainage and land recovery, and has already disappeared from some places and is threatened in others.

This species occurs throughout central and southern Europe and extends eastwards into southern Russia. Its most northerly location is in southern Sweden, and it is scattered in several other parts of northern Europe. As yet it has not been recorded from the British Isles but in the Channel Islands a very closely-related species *Orchis laxiflora* Lam., the Jersey Orchid or Loose-flowered Orchid, is still found in considerable quantities. This plant is also found in several places in southern Europe.

O. laxiflora

root tubers of *Dactylorhiza* and *Orchis* species

Orchis spitzelii

Saut. (*spitzelii*: after A. von Spitzel, who discovered the species in 1853)

In a country whose flora has been well researched, the discovery of a new species arouses a great deal of attention. In 1939 there was a sensation in Sweden when a well-known botanist, Bengt Pettersson, discovered an orchid which was new to Sweden. At first he described it as a local variety of *Orchis spitzelii*, but observed later that the Swedish colony was virtually identical with the southern European colonies. This species does, in fact, have its main distribution in the mountain regions of southern Europe, and the site in Sweden represents an isolated northern outpost. No explanation as to how this plant came north has yet been provided. One possibility is that the species was unknowingly brought in by a human agency, possibly as seeds; another is that it formerly had a much wider distribution in Europe and that this extended to Sweden.

The casual observer could confuse *Orchis spitzelii* with the Early Purple Orchid *O. mascula*. This is certainly one of the reasons why it was overlooked for so long in Sweden; one day it might even be discovered in the British Isles. The flowers of this species are characterized by their conical spurs directed downwards and the perianth which forms a helmet and is heavily tinged with green. The inflorescence does not, therefore, shine with such a bright red-violet as the Early Purple. It is cylindrical with clearly protruding flowers that tend to turn in one direction. The pale red-violet lip hangs straight down. All-white flowers are occasionally seen. Another diagnostic feature is that *O. spitzelii* comes into flower somewhat later than *O. mascula*.

During the last decade, the species has become much more widespread in many parts of Europe simply because it is better known and assiduously hunted by amateur naturalists. It is found in abundance particularly near the sea-shore where there are scattered pine trees, and it grows alongside dry heathland plants such as the bearberry (*Arctostaphylos uva-ursi*). Otherwise, it is generally found on dry limey ground at roadsides, rock-strewn ground, uncultivated fields and in open woods. It seems to do well where there has been draining, clearing and where grazing has been discontinued. The much-discussed clearing and salting of roads should have a beneficial effect on the propagation of what was formerly Europe's rarest *Orchis* species.

The distribution of *Orchis spitzelii* extends from Scandinavia to southern Europe – from Spain in the west to Turkey in the east. Sites are therefore very wide apart, which indicates the evident stability of the species and its ability to survive over a long period.

bearberry

Orchis mascula

(L.) L.   (*mascula*: male)

Early Purple Orchid

As early as April, woodlands all over the British Isles are
red-violet or pink-purple. The Early Purple Orchid, our
earliest flowering orchid, grows in abundance in all but the
most mountainous and urban areas. Sometimes they can
be seen by the thousands, while another year there may be
only a few. In fact, the plant very often dies after flowering.
Development from seed to plant takes several years, and it is
evident when the seed has set badly. It is natural that this
orchid, which is very common but most irregular in its
flowering, has been named in many European countries after
the legendary St Peter.

St Peter's Spikes, as it is called in Scandinavia, has a fairly
stout, slightly purple stalk. The leaves, arranged almost like a
rosette, can be pure dark green or with black-red spots. The
numerous flowers are gathered into a somewhat spread-out
spike. The outer perianth is set upwards and backwards. The
lip is long and hangs down, while the spur points upwards.
The flower colours vary more than in most other *Orchis*,
ranging from bright purple to bright pink or pure white. The
lip with its dark specks is brighter, as a rule, than the flower.
Even the scent can vary. Usually it is unpleasant (cat's urine),
but sometimes colonies occur which have a pleasant vanilla
scent. The flowers are pollinated by bees and bumble-bees.
The pollination procedure is highly sophisticated (see p. 14).

The Early Purple Orchid grows mainly on calcareous soils
but has often been found on neutral or even slightly acidic
ones. It occurs in rough pastures, on cliffs, open downland,
in woodlands, and sometimes at the edge of marshes. In the
British Isles it is especially common in coppiced woodlands.

Orchis mascula occurs all over Europe but in the most
northerly locations it is confined to the coastal regions. Outside of Europe it extends to North Africa and into western
Asia. Hybrids with several other *Orchis* species have sometimes been encountered.

Orchis pallens L. (*pallens*: pale, yellowish) is a very rare
species which occurs mainly in southern Europe, but which
also grows in parts of Germany. It has strongly scented
yellow flowers interspersed with broad, green, spear-shaped
leaves. It grows in meadows and open deciduous woods.

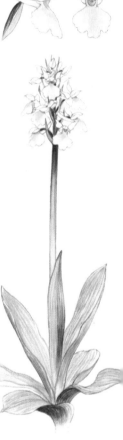

O. pallens

Orchis morio

L. (*morio*: crazy)

Green-winged Orchid

Some fifty to one hundred years ago the Green-winged Orchid was very common, possibly the most common plant over large stretches of southern and central Europe, including much of England, Wales and Ireland. Under the right conditions tens of thousands of flowers appeared in one area and coloured the fields purple-red. In some parts of Europe, particularly in the south, it continues to be abundant in certain areas but has begun to disappear in others, most noticeably in parts of central Europe and the British Isles. The species has almost died out in large areas, probably as the result of new methods of cultivation and the intensive use of artificial fertilizers.

The Green-winged Orchid is a short plant with a fairly stout stalk surrounded by a number of sheath-like leaves. At the base there are several normal leaves with oblong, grey-green shoots formed in a rosette shape. The inflorescence is widely spaced and looks as if it has been cut off at the top. The sepals and petals are helmet-like. An old Scandinavian name is Clown Spikes which refers to this helmet which is not unlike a clown's cap. The spur is divided at the point and is often held almost horizontally. The flower colours can vary a great deal. Normally the basic colour is purplish-red, but frequently we find white-flowered forms in which there is no red pigmentation. The veins of the petals and sepals are always a rich green and usually the saddle-shaped lip has a dark-spotted centre.

Orchis morio flowers as early as late April or as late as late June. The flowers are pollinated by bees and bumble-bees. There is no free nectar in the spur. The plant does well where there is low vegetation on both damp and dry open ground, and on meadows and fields, often growing alongside Cowslips (*Primula veris*) in lime-rich soils.

The Green-winged Orchid, found throughout Europe, extends east into the Near East and south to North Africa. It is still widespread over the British Isles but is never seen in the quantities previously recorded. Hybrids between the Early Purple and the Green-winged Orchids (*Orchis × morioides* Brand.) have been reliably reported from several localities.

Orchis ustulata

L. (*ustulata*: burnt)

Burnt Orchid

During his journey in Sweden Linnaeus wrote: 'The Orchis Militaris Minima is called here the Gun Powder Burner, a name that is exceptionally well chosen since the spike has red flowers as well as fire, and at the top, small unprotruding black flowers, which are built round the flame'. The Latin name is the basis of most European local names for the plant. The 'Gun Powder Burner' or Burnt Orchid as it is usually called in Britain is therefore easy to recognize by the striking contrast between the colours on the spike and the almost black flowers at the top. It is a small orchid with a very slender stalk, at the bottom of which there are usually three broad short leaves bent outwards. The growth pattern of this plant is unique. A mycorrhizome, which grows over a period of ten years, provides the growing plant with food through its fungus partner. The rhizome is then replaced with root tubers and roots (see p. 16).

fruiting stem

The inflorescence is a compact cylindrical spike with a rounded top. The perianth on the flower forms a helmet. Initially it is brown-violet, but later on a bright red to red-violet, with the lower flowers becoming pale red. The divided lip has regularly-arranged red spots on its white-pink base. The flower colours seem to be consistent throughout the species. Flowering takes place during June. The strong and sweetly scented flowers are visited by a variety of insects, but the most regular pollinator is not yet identified.

Orchis ustulata grows singly or in groups and develops best on dry, open, chalky or limestone ground. It also grows on sandy and gravelly ground and seems to need short grass for its development. It is seldom found in woodland or among shrubs. The Burnt Orchid is among those which have been heavily reduced in numbers within large areas of its field of distribution since much grassland and meadowland has been subjected to drainage, ploughing and other forms of agricultural 'improvement'. Undergrazing also can lead to its local extinction.

Orchis ustulata has been recorded from many parts of Europe but has always been one of the more local species in its distribution. It is found in several places in England but it must now be regarded as one of our rarest species.

Orchis purpurea

Huds. (*purpurea*: purple)

Lady Orchid

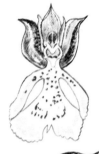

In England the Lady Orchid is abundant in Kent, but is almost never found in any other area. This largest and most spectacular of the *Orchis* species resembles a tropical orchid in its majestic size and colourful flowers. In flower colour it resembles a gigantic form of the Burnt Orchid and it also has some similarities to its near relative the Military Orchid.

The stout stalk can grow to a height of over one metre under the best conditions and has a collection of broad, bright green leaves shaped like a rosette at its base. The leaves, like the flowers, have a faint scent of freshly-mown hay. The long cylindrical inflorescence is rounded with its flowers packed together at the top, but they are more widely separated at the bottom. They become even more widely separated as flowering continues, and the lower withering flowers and fruit grow even more far apart in the middle of the stalk. The brown-violet to purple petals and sepals close like a lid or helmet around the column. The white or pale red-violet, cyclamen-coloured lip is trilobed. Its groups of purple-red hairs (papillae) make the lip look as if it is covered with dark spots. The lip varies greatly in shape: the central lobe is sometimes complete, sometimes consists of small lobes, or may be almost curly and wrinkled, and looks like a lady with a crinoline or very wide skirt.

The Lady Orchid comes into flower in early summer. Little is known of the pollination mechanism but research indicates that the flowers only pollinate sporadically and seed formation is poor. The plant only does well on chalky soil, and grows most abundantly in open clearings in deciduous woods, often beech, as well as in woodland margins, scrubland and in thickets. Sometimes it is found in open downland, in old fields which support a rich growth of plants. As a basically woodland plant, it should be one of the orchids favoured by planned reforestation.

In Scandinavia the Lady Orchid is found in only a few places in Denmark, which is its northernmost limit. It occurs mainly to the south, being widespread in southern and central Europe down to the Mediterranean. It also grows in the Caucasus, Asia Minor and North Africa. Its distribution is similar to that of the Military Orchid, and hybrids between the two species occur very often. Hybrids have also been reported, perhaps appropriately, between the Lady Orchid and the Man Orchid (*Aceras anthropophorum*); their Latin name is × *Orchiaceras macra* (Lindl.) Camus.

114–115

Orchis militaris

L.   (*militaris*: soldier, wearing a helmet [the flower])

Military Orchid

A group of fully-grown Military Orchids is a wonderful sight. It is doubtful whether this orchid attains such a size and has such beautiful flowers anywhere in the northern outposts except on some Swedish islands. Its Swedish name of Johannes Spikes is said to be associated with St John's night (Midsummer Night) since it is around midsummer that the flowers are at their best.

The Military Orchid has large oval tubers and a tall powerful stalk. A number of broad, thick, bright green unspotted leaves with clear veins grow around the base. Two sheath-like leaves surround the stalk. The multi-floral, broad, oval inflorescence looks rather dull until the flowers, with their contrasting colours, open out. The outside of the outer perianth is dull grey-violet or grey-red, but the inside is a brighter violet and reddish purple with transparent veins. The Latin name of the plant indicates that the perianth is folded and cup-shaped, resembling a knight's helmet with open visor. The flower lip is roughly the same shape as in the Burnt Orchid, resembling a body with outstretched limbs. Its paler central lobe has reddish-purple hairs or papillae. The short spur is bent. Bees and flies can be seen on the sweet-scented flowers. It is not clear to what extent these insects are really pollinators.

fruiting stem

The Military Orchid grows on chalky soil in damp meadows or dry heathland and in woods, even planted ones. It easily establishes itself on new ground, and quickly spreads to restored arable land or to areas no longer used for pasture. It also thrives on cultivated land beside roads and in ditches.

In northern Europe, the Military Orchid is concentrated mainly in Sweden where here and there very large numbers can be seen. At one time it was fairly frequently encountered in southern England, especially in the Thames Valley region, but the change of agricultural methods and over-picking of the handsome flowers has made it one of our rarest species. At the present time it occurs on one site in Suffolk and in two or three places in the Chilterns. It is, however, one of the most common orchids in the chalk and limestone regions of central Europe. It can also be found over large areas of the rest of Europe with its northernmost limits in the chalk regions around the Baltic. It extends eastwards to Lake Baikal.

Orchis simia

Lam. (*simius*: monkey)

Monkey Orchid

This very rare British orchid acquired its name because parts of the flower look like a little spider monkey. The 'body' is made up of the lobed lip with two narrow lobes at its base, the 'arms', with a short central lobe, the 'tail'. All the lobes are white at the base and red-violet at the extremities. The upper perianths envelop the column, the monkey's 'head'. The petals and sepals, which come together to form a hood, are white to pale violet with dark stripes and dots. The lip's central lobe is somewhat spotted with small red-violet tufts of hair. Pure white flowers occur only rarely.

An unusual feature of this orchid is that the flowers open first at the top of the compact, rounded and short cluster. In southern Europe the flowers bloom in April and May, but in the latter part of May and early June in the northern areas. The flowers have a faint scent of newly-cut hay (a smell of coumarin). Very little is known about how the flowers are pollinated, but it is probably mostly by bees.

The Monkey Orchid can grow to a good height, sometimes up to half a metre or more. The stem has five or six dark green to pure green leaves. The lower ones are broad and oval, while the upper ones are narrower and encircle the stem.

This orchid prefers chalky or neutral soil, especially if the ground is sandy and somewhat dry. It does well in very open grassland, the edges of woods and open scrubland. In southern Europe it is often found on mountain slopes.

Orchis simia is very similar to *O. militaris*, *O. purpurea* and *O. ustulata*. All these orchids have narrow bracts near the flowers and the petals and sepals are more or less closed, rather like a hood or helmet. Hybrids involving all these species have been reported, the most frequently encountered being *Orchis × beyrichii* A. Kern. (*O. simia × O. militaris*).

The Monkey Orchid is found in parts of western and central Europe, from Belgium and England in the north to the Mediterranean area and parts of southern Russia, Asia Minor and Iran. In England, however, it is a very rare species, found only in a few localities in the Chiltern Hills and in Kent.

Neotinea maculata

(Desf.) Stearn   (*neo*: new, *Tinea*: genus named after Tineo, a nineteenth-century professor of botany in Palermo, *maculata*: spotted)

Dense-flowered Orchid

This orchid, the only species in the genus, has a unique distribution. It is actually a typical Mediterranean type, but has outposts in the Isle of Man and in the limestone regions of western Ireland, where there is an unusually rich and varied flora. It is possible that it has been overlooked in other places. The distribution is explained by the fact that when the climate was warmer it was more widely distributed, but it still remains in pockets where the ocean brings a warm climate and the soil conditions are favourable.

The Dense-flowered Orchid, sometimes found with the Lesser Butterfly Orchid, has rather egg-shaped underground tubers. From the shoot which has survived the winter, a stalk grows up to 30 cm with a very small compact flower cluster. In the regions where the species is most widely distributed, the leaves are generally covered with purple spots. The Irish form usually has unmarked leaves. The two or three lower leaves are large, wide and tongue-shaped. The top of the stem is surrounded by a number of narrower pale green leaves.

The blooms of the elegant inflorescence are very close together and point irregularly in one direction. On close examination, the small pale violet-pink, white and green flowers are particularly beautiful. The pink and white tongue is in three parts with a somewhat wider central lobe. There is a short spur-like formation. The other perianths form a forward-leaning hood with clearly protruding and strongly coloured veins. This orchid flowers early, usually in April and the beginning of May. Little is known about its pollination, but self-pollination seems to be most likely.

In the Mediterranean region this orchid generally grows in the macchie thickets or in evergreen, oak or pine woods near the coast. It also grows on rocky or stony soil, and in Ireland on fields where the soil is predominantly limestone. The southern orchids seem to be able to exist in northerly areas on warm limestone near the coast. The total distribution extends to the western parts of southern Europe, the Mediterranean region, North Africa, Madeira and the Canary Islands.

Anacamptis pyramidalis

(L.) Rich. (*anakampto*: to bend upwards, *pyramidalis*: pyramid-shaped)

Pyramidal Orchid

Salep is a pharmaceutical term for the mucilage derived from the root tubers of many orchids. Salep comes from an Arabic word which means 'testicles of a fox'. Salep mucilage was used in Britain at one time to relieve itching. In the East it was thought to enhance virility. Our native 'Salep Root' as it was once called, has had a limited use in medicine. It is a characteristic, richly-coloured orchid which grows best in a warm dry environment. The genus *Anacamptis* is closely related to *Orchis* and also has spherical root tubers. The slender stalk, which grows to about 45 cm, has short leaves and at its base there are larger spear-shaped leaves. The compact inflorescence forms a broad, short, rounded pyramid. The flowers are strong reds, violets or purples but rarely white. It has a pleasant scent, but contains no free nectar. The dorsal sepal and the two petals form a cover above the broad trilobed lip. The lip has two upright ridges or folds and a long thread-like spur. The flowers are shaped so that they can only be pollinated by butterflies. This is one of many examples of evolution. Because of the fold in the flower's lip the butterfly must insert its proboscis as if through a tunnel, straight into the flower. The pollinia are attached by a common, saddle-shaped sticky disc contained in a pouch-like space. The sticky disc attaches itself to the insect's proboscis (see illustration in the margin). The pollinia are then bent forward into a position where they come in contact with the two stigmas when a visit is paid to another flower. The butterfly obtains nectar by breaking apart the cells in the thick-walled spur.

The Pyramidal Orchid blooms at the height of the summer but flowers only appear after five to ten years' growth. During this time the plant is heavily dependent on its mycorrhizal fungus. The leaf and shoot survive the winter. It seems to prefer, or depend on, cultivation – grazing and hay fields – and grows best on open grassland. It will quickly colonize new grassland and abandoned pasture and is frequent in calcareous sand dunes. Even if the plant sometimes grows in open woods and thickets it can be threatened if there is reforestation. The Pyramidal Orchid is a south Eurasian variety which extends over southern and central Europe, North Africa and western Asia. In the British Isles *Anacamptis pyramidalis* is widespread except in Scotland. However, it is commonest in southern England where it can form large populations.

fruiting stem

122–123

Himantoglossum hircinum

(L.) Spreng. (*himas*: belt, rein, *glossa*: heavy, *hircinus*: goat)

Lizard Orchid

The Lizard Orchid is one of Europe's most peculiar orchids. It is a large, odd-looking plant which, when not in full flower, hardly resembles an orchid. When the plant is in flower, however, the long, ribbon-like twisted central lobe on the lip is particularly noticeable. The lip is trilobed with two short side lobes and a long central one which, initially, is coiled like a clock spring. The curly lip carries small papillae and hairs at its base. The upper perianths form a cover above the lip. The spur is short. The flower is grey to pale green with streaks of purple to brownish purple. The flowers form a compact, large, long cluster.

The plant has acquired many popular names based on the strange appearance of the flower. Lizard and Tadpole Orchid are frequent names. Each individual flower does, in fact, resemble a small lizard or a tadpole. The Swedish name of Goat Orchid refers to the unusual rancid goat-like smell which attracts flies, bees and sometimes bluebottles.

The underground parts of the plant consist of oval or spool-shaped tubers. The strong stalk is surrounded by very large leaves, the lower ones being wide, long and pointed. The lowest leaves are formed during the autumn and survive the winter but often wither during flowering.

The plant grows in sunny, open and grass-covered ground, on the edges of woods or shrubs and in open woods. It can also appear on sand dunes in western Europe, and seems to favour an oceanic climate. In southern Europe the flowers appear in April, and in northern Europe in June or July. The plant is found mostly in the south and is fairly common in parts of southern Europe, but grows only sporadically in central and northern Europe. It extends in a northerly direction to southeast England, southern Holland, southwest Germany, Czechoslovakia and parts of Austria. In England it is now very rare, confined to a very few localities in the southeast, but fifty or so years ago it suddenly spread to many places throughout southern England and was reported as far west as Gloucestershire and Somerset. The *Himantoglossum* found around the eastern Mediterranean seems to be a sub-species or variety called *caprinum*.

In very restricted areas of southeast Europe (Yugoslavia) there is another species, *H. calcaratum*.

Aceras anthropophorum

(L.) Ait. f. (*aceras*: without horn or spur, *anthropophorum*: of human form)

Man Orchid

Many orchids have taken their names – both Latin and local – from the similarity of the flowers to a human or animal body. It is not only botanists who have discovered in amazement how orchids are constructed: in the case of the Man Orchid, it is not only the flower shape, but the pale yellowish to brownish green colour.

The genus *Aceras* is very close to *Orchis*, especially *O. purpurea*, *O. simia* and *O. militaris* with which it occasionally forms hybrids. The flowers, however, have similar spurs. The underground parts consist of oval tubers and thick roots. The broad lower leaves of the stalk are tongue-shaped, with rounded ends, while the upper ones are pointed and encircle the stalk. The flower cluster is long and quite narrow.

The lip of the flower is shaped like a body with lobes resembling 'trunk', 'arms' and 'legs'. It hangs straight down and the lobes are yellow to red-brown or yellow-brown with green streaks. The upper perianth forms, at the same time, a hood of a paler colour. The flowers have a faint and somewhat unpleasant smell, and occasionally the scent, as with the Monkey and Military Orchids, resembles coumarin. Particularly when they are dry, there is a faint scent of freshly-cut hay. Many small insects such as flies visit the flowers, but pollination details have not been fully reported.

The Man Orchid is one of the plants which prefer lime and chalk, and is usually found on the edges of forests, in open scrubland, wooded fields and mountain forests, as well as on grassy banks in limestone quarries. It is a particularly persistent species, occurring often even where public trampling pressure is especially great, as on the chalk hills in Surrey, south of London.

It is distributed over large parts of Europe, from England and West Germany in the north to North Africa in the south. The Man Orchid is fairly common where it occurs in England but it is confined to the south central, southeast and areas of the west. It is not very common in eastern Europe, especially in southern Greece and in Asia Minor, and it is also uncommon in the most northerly parts of its habitat. In recent years it has vanished from many of its sites after they have been cultivated or built on. In some areas it has re-occupied land which was at one time under cultivation. It may, therefore, like many other orchids, prefer low scrub.

Chamorchis alpina

(L.) L. C. Rich. (*kaamai*: on the ground or low down, *alpina*: alpine)

False Musk Orchid

One of Europe's smallest and more inconspicuous orchids, False Musk lives in an unusual environment. It is found only in the mountains of Scandinavia and the alpine regions of the Continent at heights between 1500 and 3000 m above sea-level. In the alpine regions it is exposed to bright sunshine during the day and frosts and biting winds at night. It is the only member of the genus *Chamorchis*. It has undivided oval root tubers and a short, strong, somewhat rectangular pale yellow-green stalk which is, in general, 3–8 cm tall. At the stalk base there are several long leaves like blades of grass. The small flowers, sometimes only two or three together, are arranged as a loose spike beside strong green bracts. The petals and sepals form a helmet or projecting cover over the lip which hangs down like a tongue, sometimes in an indistinctly trilobed shape and sometimes notched. The yellow-green lip has a darker green slit. There is no spur. The flowers are green with brown or purple markings. The False Musk Orchid has no scent but is visited by a variety of small, typical alpine insects. It is thought that the flowers are usually self-pollinated. The closed withered flowers remain for a long time on the fruit formation. *Chamorchis alpina* is an alpine plant requiring chalk, and it generally occurs in small colonies, principally on the bare mountains. It is often found in heathland in the lower and central Alps where it grows typically among such plants as *Dryas octopetala* (Mountain Avens). The False Musk Orchid is also found on the rocky slopes formed after landslides where it thrives alongside the Edelweiss (*Leontopodium alpinum*). In high places it can be found on exposed heathland where there is hardly any other vegetation in a climate consisting mainly of rain, frost and wind. In Sweden where *Chamorchis alpina* is rather rare, it extends especially to the regions of Lapland with occurrences down to northern Härjedal. In Norway it is found in the high mountains as far as the North Cape, and in Finland there is one known site. Outside Scandinavia it is found in the mountain regions of Europe, the Alps, Carpathians and mountains of the Baltic. It is also known to exist in the Kola Peninsula. On the Continent, where it seldom grows below levels of 1500 m above sea-level, it can sometimes be found in colonies of up to a hundred plants.

Ophrys insectifera

L. (*ophrys*: eyebrow, *insectifera*: carrying insects)

Fly Orchid

Many plants have extraordinarily ingenious arrangements for the adaptation to pollinators and the animal-plant symbiotic relationship. Among the more unusual are those of the genus *Ophrys* whose brightly coloured and unusually shaped flowers resemble insects. Four species of *Ophrys* are found in the British Isles but most plants belong to the Mediterranean area and comprise a bewildering array of strains, races, forms, varieties, sub-species and hybrids.

The Fly Orchid has no striking inflorescence, and the plant often merges with the surrounding vegetation. Only when examining it more closely does one see the very curious shape and colour of the flowers, sitting like a row of insects on the pale green stalk.

The outer green sepals may pass unnoticed; it is the other parts which make up the 'insect'. The two small brown petals resemble antennae and the 'body' is made up of the folded lip. It looks as if it is covered in deep red-brown velvet with a gleaming metallic blue spot or strip in the middle. The column makes up the 'head'.

The flowers, without a spur or free nectar, have an odour which acts like a female sex scent for the males of two wasp species belonging to the *Gorytes* and *Argogorytes* genera. One of them, *G. mystaceus*, seems to visit the plant soon after it has flowered, the other, *G. campestris*, later on. The male is attracted by the scent from the flower lip; when he lands on it the scent and hair structure, which are strikingly like the female's, stimulate him to make mating motions. During these abortive copulatory movements the insect reaches the pollinia which attach themselves to its head. The pollinia then point forwards into a position from which they come in contact with the stigma of another flower (see pp. 14 and 15). This pollination mechanism is called pseudocopulation.

The Fly Orchid grows on calcareous soils in marshes, open fields and especially in woodland margins. Reforestation and draining have caused it to disappear or become rare in a number of places. Its total distribution covers much of Europe, but there are some areas where it is very rare or even absent, although this may be due partly to its being overlooked. In the British Isles it is scattered over the southern half but is not really common anywhere.

Ophrys sphegodes

Muell.   (*ophrys*: eyebrow, *sphegodes*: relative of the solitary bee)

Early Spider Orchid

The fascinating and complicated interaction between plant and insect in the genus *Ophrys* is highly developed in the many forms found in the Mediterranean region where the genus is most widely distributed. The dependence of many *Ophrys* species on certain bee species for its pollination is thought to be the result of a step-by-step parallel evolution. The *Ophrys* flowers have become adapted to the copulatory instincts of the male bee for pollination. It is assumed that the rich variations in colour and shape within this well-defined and typical strain mean that the strain is young and genetically unstable. Although there are various factors that determine the relationship between plant and pollinator, the most important seems to be the attraction either of scent or the biologically active substance given off by the flower for certain insects. Other factors are the shape of the flower and the manner in which pollination is carried out. The bees, the main pollinators among the *Ophrys* found around the Mediterranean, are in a way related to *Andrena* and *Eucera*.

The rich variations in colour and shape of the *Ophrys* in the Mediterranean area make it difficult to make a systematic record of the genus. Opinions on the number of species in the family are varied, and the number of species reported varies from sixteen to around thirty. A very large number of sub-species, varieties and shapes have been described. It is hoped that current research on the family's complicated pollination procedures will shed some light on relationships.

Apart from the Fly Orchid, three other species are found in northern parts of Europe. The Early Spider Orchid, which grows mostly in southern and central Europe, is also found occasionally in southern England and central Germany. This type can grow to a height of about 50 cm. The stem is surrounded by a number of broad, spear-shaped, grey-green leaves. The brown, large and almost round tongue covered with brown hairs resembles the body of a thick spider. Its colours vary considerably. The bright and bald part, usually in the shape of an H, is blue or blue-violet. The outer perianth is green to greenish white and the inner ones are yellow-green or brown olive green.

The flowers open as early as April. Pollination is usually by the sand bee of the *Andrena* family. Differently scented substances are emitted by the different types in this large family which is, so far, not fully researched.

The Early Spider Orchid grows almost exclusively on chalky open fields among short species of grass. The family seems to favour cultivated areas but has become rare in many of its northern habitats where there has been recultivation.

132–133

Ophrys fuciflora

(Crantz) Moench. (*fuciflora*: having red or purple flowers)

Late Spider Orchid

This lovely species has, in recent years, become rarer in the northern outposts of its habitats because its usual sites are being disturbed. It can sometimes be found in a few places along the south coast of England, particularly in Kent.

O. fuciflora
ssp. *fuciflora*

The Late Spider Orchid has the most fantastic and beautiful variations in flower colour and lip formation. The short broad sepals vary from violet-pink to red-purple, but can be white with various shades of green. The much smaller inner petals have similar colour variations. The thick, hairy brown lip is broadly rectangular or somewhat rounded to heart-shaped, and has an upright, sometimes divided, point which is usually a shade of yellow. The bare part of the lip is often brown to brown-violet (or blue-violet) and varies in appearance. It is generally surrounded by brighter, almost white edges and spots, like a kind of collar. There may be one or more circular parts edged by a white ring.

The stem, which in rare cases can grow to half a metre in height, has a rosette of broad leaves at the base. The flower cluster has only a few widely-spaced flowers, sometimes only one or two. The plant flowers at the end of May and during June, but somewhat earlier in southern Europe. The flowers, with a faint cyclamen scent, are typical of most *Ophrys* species, pollinated by the solitary male bee of the *Eucera* species. Occasionally, however, the pollinator is a male of the genus *Tetralonia*. The volatile substance emitted by the lip of this and other types of *Ophrys* flower has been examined with the aid of gas chromotography, and has been found to be a derivative of fatty acids and terpenes. It seems that self-pollination can occur. It seems likely that some types can pollinate themselves, but at the same time retain their adaptation to the male bee.

two southern
European variants

The Late Spider Orchid is generally found in chalky soil and in open grass fields, even if they are stony or sandy. It also grows in open pine woods and on open mountainsides where there are bushes and trees. The distribution is mainly in the Mediterranean region but reaches central Germany in the north. Eastwards it extends to the eastern Mediterranean and Syria.

Ophrys apifera

Huds. (*apifera*: resembling a bee or bumble-bee)

Bee Orchid

This is a delightfully coloured and beautifully marked orchid.
The three white or pale pink to bright reddish-violet broad
sepals contrast sharply with the thick, pouch-like, red-brown,
hairy lip with its pattern of bright edges and spots. The lip
has two conical, very hairy, side lobes and a yellowish curved
point. The small inner petals are often a shade of green. As
with most species of *Ophrys*, there are numerous colour and
marking variations. Some specimens have an imperfectly
formed, pointed, wasp-like lip and are sometimes distinguished as a distinct variety, var. *trollii* (Hegetschw.) Druce
(Wasp Orchid). Plants without red shades in their flowers,
and consequently only white and green, are var. *chlorantha*
Godf. Flowering occurs in southern Europe in April and
May and in central and northern Europe in June and July.
Self-pollination can easily occur as the pollinia's stem comes
together and pulls out the pollinia, so that they hang loose.
A puff of wind can then easily bring them into contact with
the stigma. Self-pollination seems to be usual in its northerly
habitats. In the Mediterranean area the species is pollinated
by solitary male bees of the *Eucera* species. One type of the
volatile substance given off by *Ophrys* flowers is limited to
species which are only pollinated by the *Eucera* bee.

This *Ophrys* species often grows to a height of about half
a metre, with a number of very wide grey-green leaves at the
stalk base which survive the winter. The plant is found in
mainly chalky areas, particularly in the northern regions. It
seems to thrive in cultivated open fields, roads, on pastureland as well as in gravel and sandy regions. In the west,
especially in England, Wales and Ireland, it is frequently
found on sand dunes. The species comes up quickly, sometimes in large colonies, only to disappear after a short time.
These population changes make it difficult to determine its
rarity.

The Bee Orchid is not as common in parts of northwest
Europe from Germany to Ireland, but in the south it is seen
over large areas of the Mediterranean and also extends eastwards to Romania and the Caucasus. It is one of the commonest orchids in the British Isles except that it is absent
from Scotland. It thrives on the chalk downs in southern
England.

Herminium monorchis

(L.) R. Br.   (*hermis*: support, *monorchis*: a single testicle [tuber])

Musk Orchid

The Musk Orchid is migratory. Its tuber, which has been storing food during the year, puts out a bud from a runner, enabling the plant to spread underground. *Herminium* is closely related to *Aceras* and *Orchis*. This orchid, sometimes only a few centimetres tall, looks more like a lily, with its angularly protruding bell-like flowers. It has no spur, and the narrow, ridged, tongue-like lip is barely separate from the rest of the flower. The yellow-green flowers have a sweet scent of honey or musk. There is no honey in the form of free nectar in the flowers, yet they are visited and pollinated by a variety of small insects such as beetles and flies. The insect crawls into the flower and supports its front legs against the unusually large saddle-shaped sticky discs. The pollinia then become attached to the insect and are taken to another flower where the pollen packet from the protruding pollinia comes into contact with the somewhat extended stigma. Because the pollen can easily fall onto the stigma, self-pollination often takes place. According to information available, self-pollination is general in some colonies.

fruiting stem

The Musk Orchid grows best in calcareous soils in open situations – fields, the sea-shore, streams and open leafy ground. It requires moist and chalky conditions. Today this species is becoming much less abundant throughout its range, but it can very easily be overlooked and trampled because it is small and its colour merges with the surroundings. It is often found in groups, and at one time it occurred in such quantities that it gave a yellow-green hue to its entire growing area. Ditching and replanting have made it rare on many of its earlier sites.

Herminium monorchis is found throughout Europe and extends as far east as Mongolia and Japan. In central Asia where it is particularly common it tends to be a high-altitude plant but elsewhere it can grow right down to sea-level. In Britain it is confined to southern England and southern Wales.

Saving our orchids: conservation legislation in the United Kingdom

Mounting concern for endangered species of plants and animals in the United Kingdom and throughout the world has resulted in two Acts of Parliament being passed to protect them. Both Acts concern orchids as well as other plants.

Although native British species are not usually exported, many rare tropical and sub-tropical species are imported into the British Isles on a large scale for commercial sale for cultivation in greenhouses. To control the trade in these plants all orchids are subject to the conditions of the *Endangered Species (Import and Export) Act 1976*. Licences are required for importing orchids into this country and can be applied for from the Department of the Environment (17/19 Rochester Row, London SW1P 1LN).

Of more relevance to British species of orchid is the *Conservation of Wild Creatures and Wild Plants Act 1975*. The major clauses relating to orchids:

If, save as may be permitted by or under this Act, any person other than an authorized person without reasonable excuse uproots any plant, he shall be guilty of an offence.

If, save as may be permitted by or under this Act, any person without reasonable excuse picks, uproots or destroys any protected plant listed in Schedule 2, he shall be guilty of an offence unless the picking, uprooting or destruction occurs as an incidental result, which could not reasonably have been avoided, of any operation which was carried out in accordance with agricultural or forestry practice.

A person shall not be guilty of an offence against this Act by reason only of the doing of anything in pursuance or furtherance of any obligation imposed, or in exercise of any powers conferred, by or under an Act of Parliament.

Where, on a representation made to him by the Nature Conservancy Council, it appears to the Secretary of State to be necessary in the interest of the proper conservation of ... plants he may by order add any ... plant to, or remove any ... plant from, ... Schedule 2 to this Act.

An order made under this subsection may apply:

(a) to the whole or to particular provisions of this Act;

(b) generally or to a particular area;

(c) to ... plants in a particular category; or

(d) at all times or at particular times of the year; and the order may make different provision for different circumstances.

A licence may be granted to any person ... subject to compliance with any specified conditions, for scientific or educational purposes or for the conservation of plants, to pick or uproot within a specified area by any specified means any plant of a specified species. The appropriate authority for the grant of a licence shall be the Nature Conservancy Council.

Any person guilty of an offence under this Act shall be liable on summary conviction to a fine not exceeding £100. Provided that, where the offence was committed ... in respect of more than one species of plant, the maximum fine which may be imposed under this subsection shall be determined as if the person convicted had been convicted of a separate offence in respect of each protected ... species of plant ...

The Nature Conservancy Council at any time may, and five years after the passing of this Act and every five years thereafter shall, review the Schedules to this Act and shall advise the Secretary of State if any ... plant has become so rare that its status as a British ... plant is being endangered by any action designated as an offence under this Act and it should be included in Schedule 2 ... either generally or with respect to a particular area or in relation to a particular category and either at all times or at particular times of the year or has become so common that its status is no longer endangered and it should be removed therefrom.

A local authority shall take such steps as they consider expedient for bringing the effect of this Act to the attention of the public and in particular schoolchildren.

A local authority in England or Wales shall have power to institute proceedings for any offence under this Act committed within their area.

Schedule 2 – Protected Plants

The twenty-one species include five orchids:

Cephalanthera rubra: Red Helleborine
Cypripedium calceolus: Lady's Slipper
Epipogium aphyllum: Ghost Orchid
Orchis militaris: Military Orchid
Orchis simia: Monkey Orchid

This Act, which covers the whole of Great Britain, means that it is now an offence, with a fine of up to £100 upon conviction, for anyone, without permission of the owner or occupier of the land or their agent, to dig up plants in the countryside. A further offence is committed if any of 21 species on Schedule 2 is picked, uprooted or destroyed.

However, the Nature Conservancy Council can issue licences for scientific, educational or conservation purposes which would make digging up or collecting of scheduled plants lawful.

Further reading

Brooke, J., *The Wild Orchids of Britain*, Bodley Head, 1950.

Camus, E. G., Bergon, P., Camus, A., *Monographie des Orchidées*, Librairie Jacques Lechevalier, Paris, 1912.

Clapham, A. R., Tutin, T. G., Warburg, E. F., *Flora of the British Isles* (pp. 1009–1050), Cambridge University Press, 1962.

Danesch, O., Danesch, E., *Orchideen Europas: Mitteleuropas: Südeurop: Ophrys Hybridien*, (3 vols), Hallwag, 1962–72.

Danesch, O., Danesch, E., *Orchideen* Hallwag Taschenbusch 114, 1975.

Duperrex, A. (trans. A. J. Huxley), *Orchids of Europe*, Blandford Press, 1961.

Ettlinger, D. M. T., *British and Irish Orchids*, Macmillan Press, 1977.

Godfery, M. J., *Monograph and Iconograph of Native British Orchidaceae*, Cambridge University Press, 1933.

Kohlhaupt, P., *Bunte Welte der Orchideen*, Franckh, 1970.

Mackenzie, J. S. E., *British Orchids: How To Tell One from Another*, Unwin Brothers, 1913.

Nelson, E., *Monographie und Ikonographie der Orchidaceen-Gattung. Serapias, Aceras, Loroglossum, Barlia; Ophrys; Dactylorhiza*, (3 vols), Verlag Speich ag Zurich, 1962–76.

Ross-Craig, S., *Drawings of British Plants*, part XXVIII, G. Bell & Sons, 1971.

Schlechter, R., Keller, G., *Monographie und Iconographie der Orchideen Europas und des Mittelmeergebiete*, Verlag des Repertoriums, Berlin, 1937–43.

Stace, C. A. (ed.), *Hybridization and the Flora of the British Isles*, (pp. 473–507), Academic Press, 1975.

Summerhayes, V. S., *Wild Orchids of Britain*, Collins, 1968.

Sundermann, H., *Europaische und Mediterrane Orchideen*, Bruke-Verlag Kurt Schmersow, 1970.

Tahourdin, C. B., *Native Orchids of Britain*, H. R. Grubb, 1925.

Webster, A. D., *British Orchids*, Virtue, 1898.

Orchid societies and journals

There are many hundreds of orchid societies throughout the world but most of these are primarily concerned with the cultivation and breeding of tropical and sub-tropical species and man-made hybrids. However, the major societies do publish occasional articles on orchids native to the society's country. In Britain the *Orchid Society of Great Britain Journal* has published some articles on native British species. The monthly *Orchid Review*, a commercially published journal dating back as far as 1893, usually has at least one popular article on British or European orchids in each issue.

The *Botanical Society of the British Isles* publishes a twice-yearly scientific journal called *Watsonia* that frequently contains articles on various aspects of orchid classification and ecology as well as shorter notes on interesting discoveries of orchids in new localities.

Many organizations, both official government bodies and voluntary societies, have been formed over the years to safeguard the environment and to conserve our wild plants and animals. One way of conserving endangered orchids is by the establishment of nature reserves in which the orchids are protected from activities such as forestry, agriculture, quarrying and sports that could harm them and possibly render them extinct. Nature reserves are established by the *Nature Conservancy Council* and by the *County Naturalists' Trusts*, of which there are now forty covering the whole of Great Britain. The activities of these Trusts are co-ordinated by the *Society for the Promotion of Nature Conservation*, which was founded in 1912 and is now the major national body concerned with conservation.

On a global scale the co-ordination of plant and wildlife conservation is carried out by the *International Union for the Conservation of Nature* (I.U.C.N.), and orchids in particular are the concern of the *Threatened Plants Committee* of the I.U.C.N.'s *Survival Service Commission*. The I.U.C.N. is financed by subscription from member states and organizations and by the *World Wildlife Fund*.

Further information on all these organizations and many others is obtainable from the *Council for Nature*, Zoological Gardens, Regents Park, London NW1 4RY.

Index

145